HOW TO *REALLY* FOOL
YOURSELF

HOW TO *REALLY* FOOL YOURSELF

ILLUSIONS FOR ALL YOUR SENSES

by

VICKI COBB

illustrated by

LESLIE MORRILL

J. B. Lippincott New York

Library of Congress Cataloging in Publication Data

Cobb, Vicki.
How to *really* fool yourself

Bibliography: p.

SUMMARY: Demonstrations accompanied by explanations
illustrate how and why the senses can be fooled.
  1. Senses and sensation—Juvenile literature.
  2. Perception—Juvenile literature. 3. Optical
illusions—Juvenile literature. [1. Senses and
sensation. 2. Perception. 3. Optical illusions]
  I. Morrill, Leslie H. II. Title.
QP434.C56   1980   612.8   79–9620
ISBN 0–397–31906–1
ISBN 0–397–31907–X (lib. bdg.)
ISBN 0–397–31908–8 (pbk.)

2 3 4 5 6 7 8 9 10

Figure on page 61 by Maurits C. Escher
Figure on page 119 by Marvin L. Minsky
and Seymour A. Papert

The author gratefully acknowledges the contributions and assistance of the following people: Dr. Edward S. Tauber and Dr. Gerald Oster for their interest and for reprints of their work in visual perception; Dr. Edward S. Cobb and Dr. Arien Mack for their critical review of the manuscript.

For Ilana and Norman Adler, who work harder than most at not kidding themselves, and for their children, David, Danny, Susan, and Jennifer.

Contents

HOW TO *REALLY* FOOL
YOURSELF

A Sense of Reality

At this very moment you are having an experience relating to this book. You are reading these words, and, if you are holding the book in your hands, you are feeling its weight and the smoothness of its pages. You may be aware of its smell. All true. So what else is new?

Seriously, how do you know that this book exists? That it is not a figment of your imagination? That it is not an illusion? In your perception, this book is real! Here's a list of reality checks to prove it:

1. You can see it.
2. You can touch it and feel its weight.
3. You can smell it and maybe taste it.
4. You can read it aloud and hear the words.
5. You can ask other people if they experience these same reality checks, thus confirming your own.

In short, you test for reality by bombarding all your senses with various aspects of the experience of this moment. If they agree, you have a sense of reality.

———A SUBJECT TO QUESTION———

What is reality, really? Three separate views of reality are nicely illustrated in the tale of three plate umpires stating how they each judged balls and strikes. The first umpire says, "I calls 'em as I sees 'em." (He trusts his sense of vision to show him what is real.) The second umpire,

feeling much superior to the first, says, "I calls 'em as they is!" (His judgments based on his sense of sight are real.) The third umpire, certain he is one up on the other two, smiles and says in resounding tones, "They ain't nothin' until I calls 'em!" (His personal judgments create reality. Where the ball actually is located in the strike zone doesn't count.)

Seriously, the question of reality has fascinated philosophers, psychologists, scientists, writers, and other seekers of truth for all of recorded history. In discussions and writings, they have considered such heavy questions as: What is existence? ("To be or not to be?") What is awareness? ("I think, therefore I am.") If a tree fell in the forest and nobody heard it, did it make a sound? These questions are fair game for anyone to argue. Try one. There is no final authority on the answers, and the solutions are still up for grabs. But as far as this book is concerned, for your experience of it and for its contents, we suggest that reality has three parts.

The first part is made up of the book's physical properties and the physical properties of the rest of the universe that are separate from you. The book's physical properties include its size, shape, weight, light reflecting from its surfaces, sounds of words read aloud, and chemical makeups of paper and ink. Physical properties to which a person responds are called *stimuli*. (A single property responded to is a *stimulus*.)

The second part of reality is *sensation*—the ways your body reacts to stimuli or events that are not separate from you. These responses occur first in specialized sense organs—eyes, ears, nose, and skin—that all have one thing in common, namely, nerve cells. Nerve cells that respond to stimuli are called *receptors*, and they carry messages of stimuli to the brain. Receptors in your eyes are, of course, sensitive to light. Vision is considered our dominant sense if you go by the numbers. Seventy percent of all receptor cells in your body are in your eyes. Sound is sensed primarily by your ears, although your skin has been known to sense certain sound vibrations. Your nose and mouth have receptors sensitive to *chemicals*. They fire messages to the brain when they make direct contact with certain molecules. Our chemical senses of smell and taste are considered our most primitive. Other animals, including dogs and fish, are far more developed in this area than we are. Basic survival in many lower animals depends more on these senses than in our case. And, finally, there is your skin and internal touch receptors, which respond to temperature, pressure, and pain in such an infinite variety of combinations that you know when a fly is walking along your

arm, when you are touching velvet, and when a pot is too hot to handle. The marvel of touch led the great philosopher Aristotle to think of it as the most important sense. For him, touch was the ultimate test of reality. If you could touch something it was truly real.

The third part of reality is knowledge gained from your past experiences. How your sense organs responded to stimuli in the past, how your brain interpreted the information, how you behaved, and the consequences of your actions all play a part in your present experience. The thousands of hours you spent learning to speak English, then learning to read it, then learning that some books are a pleasant experience, are no small part of the reality of this moment. (We hope!)

——ABOUT FOOLING YOURSELF——

Perception is the awareness that comes from the stimuli of the physical world, your sensation of them, and your experience in interpreting them. Perception is your basic way of knowing reality. But, although your perceptions *seem* accurate, they are often subject to weaknesses and limits. These make you susceptible to illusions, to *not* experiencing reality accurately, yet experiencing something that appears and feels very real. When you are aware of a misperception, you feel strange. Your mind tells you that your senses are deceiving you. The word "illusion" comes from a Latin root meaning "mockery." Your eyes and ears can play tricks on you. So can your other senses.

This is what this book is about: ways to explore the weaknesses and limits of your perception, ways to create all kinds of illusions for yourself, setting up contradictory situations where your senses tell you one message and your brain tells you another. There are many reasons why illusions occur. Some are caused by built-in limits of your senses. Some are based on conflicts between senses. Some come from false expectations. And some are in the physical world itself.

If there is any lesson to be learned in life experience, it is that we can make mistakes. Judgments based on false perceptions can be errors. (Unfortunately, they can also prove correct.) The experiments in fooling yourself in this book show one important thing: most of us perceive in similar ways, and our perceptions are similarly leading us astray. These illusions and experiments on yourself can be experienced by all of us. Sometimes it can take a little time and practice to experience them. So, if you don't "get" an illusion right away, keep trying.

Through the history of science, it has been extremely useful to know how we can be fooled. By knowing our weaknesses and limitations, we created tools to correct and extend them. Instruments like the telescope and microscope clearly extend the limits of our senses. Computers have memories that make no mistakes when it comes to total recall. Great minds create models of never-seen objects like atoms and molecules that explain events we do experience. Such ideas create another reality that helps us to understand the universe and leads to a different kind of truth. Awareness of how we can be mistaken helps us stop kidding ourselves.

Maybe our biggest illusion is that we must be right all the time. If so, you've come to the right place. This book is an adventure in human failing. Prepare yourself for many humbling yet enlightening experiences. Enjoy!

Weird Feelings

Aristotle (384–322 B.C.), the Greek philosopher, was the first to state that the human body had only five senses. He called our fifth sense "touch," although he wasn't sure that this was

a single sense like sight, hearing, smell, and taste. Modern thought on touch has come up with so many subdivisions and qualities that understanding this sense is difficult if not confusing. Some of these qualities include pressure, contact, deep pressure, muscle strain, prickly pain, deep pain, quick pain, warmth, cold, dizziness, hunger, thirst, itch, tickle, and vibration.

More than two thousand years after Aristotle, touch is still our most mysterious sense. Unlike our other senses, which have specific locations within our bodies, touch is located in two square yards of skin and in deeper underlying muscles and organs. Scientists have isolated and studied four different kinds of nerves in our skin that seem to be individually sensitive to warmth, cold, pressure, and pain, although there is some confusion as to which nerves are responsible for which feelings. The most popular current theory about touch is that the different qualities are the result of different patterns of nerve firings. A nerve firing is measured in laboratories as an electrical impulse along a nerve fiber. Different kinds of stimuli cause different receptors to fire. Different combinations of nerve firings produce different sensations. Despite the tremendous amount of research on touch done in the last hundred years, most researchers agree that we are only beginning to perceive the depth of our ignorance.

Where we have some understanding, we'll tell you about it. Where an explanation is still waiting to be discovered, we just present the illusion. Perhaps you can dream up your own experiments to explore these mysteries. Often what seems to be an explanation is perhaps just another description of what's happening. One thing, however, is certain: the experiments and illusions in this chapter will make you feel that what's happening is pretty weird.

———ARISTOTLE'S ILLUSION———

We'll begin with an illusion Aristotle discovered and which is named for him. You will *feel* two noses on your face despite your firm conviction that you only have one.

Cross your index and middle finger of your favorite hand. Run the tips of your crossed fingers up and down your nose so that the side of each finger touches one side of your nose. Feel the space between your "noses" get wider, especially toward the tip. Closing your eyes helps.

This belongs to a class of illusions called "misplaced assumptions." You are used to knowing where your fingertips are when you feel things. When you cross your fingertips, you change their

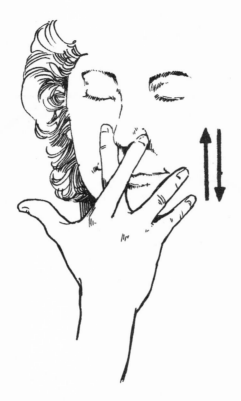

ordinary relationship to each other, and your brain is confused. You interpret the sensation as if your fingers were in their usual position.

There are variations on this. Feel a marble with crossed fingers or run them up and down a pencil. You will feel two of everything you touch. Put your index finger next to a friend's. Feel both fingers with your other hand by running your index finger and thumb along their length. You expect to feel something different from what you are actually feeling, but we can't explain just what that is.

——GIVE YOURSELF A LIFT——

In this illusion you feel as if your body has a will of its own. Your arms will rise from your shoulders without your consciously moving a muscle. Motion that normally takes some effort becomes effortless.

To give yourself a basis for comparison, stand up and raise both arms outward from your sides. Feel their weight and the strain in your muscles.

Here's how to create the illusion of weightlessness in your arms. Stand in a doorway, your hands hanging down, your palms facing your body. Move your hands outward and press the backs of your hands against the door frame. Strain your muscles as you press hard and count slowly to thirty. Your arms will shake a little with the effort.

At the end of the count step forward away from the doorway and let your arms relax completely by your sides. Your arms will rise as if you were going to take off in flight without any work on your part.

Your muscles contract as if you are actually raising your arms, although the doorway prevents your arms from actually rising. When you

step forward, you remove the obstacle, but your muscles continue to contract, thus raising your arms. This effect is like the persistent afterimage of vision (see chapter 7).

If you lift a heavy weight and then lift a light one, your judgment about how heavy the second weight is will have been altered by the previous experience. The second weight will seem much lighter. For this reason baseball players swing several bats while warming up. When they step up to the plate, the single bat will seem so much lighter by comparison that they will swing it more quickly, thus giving the ball more impact if they connect.

──────LIGHTWEIGHT THINKING──────

Consider this question: Which weighs more— a pound of feathers or a pound of gold? Most people are fooled by this riddle and answer "a pound of gold" because gold seems "heavier" (it's actually denser) than feathers. The illusion is that a smaller object feels heavier than a larger one when both are the same weight.

Check it out for yourself. We picked two items from the pantry—a small metal container of ground ginger and a box of instant onion soup. They weighed exactly the same on our postal scale. Any two items of significantly different sizes that weigh the same will do. Everyone who lifted both said that the metal box was heavier.

Here's an explanation. Your experience has taught you that, in general, smaller objects

weigh less than larger ones. You expect the smaller object to be lighter than the larger one. When you lift both, your expectations are not

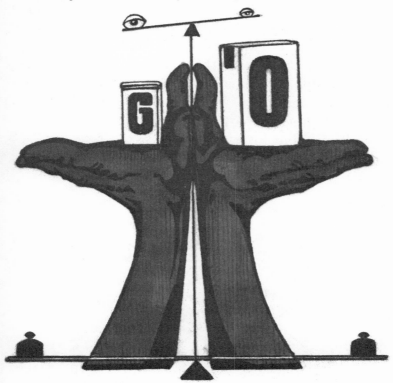

met, and the result is that the smaller object feels heavier. This explanation has its problems, however. The illusion persists even when you know that they are the same weight and when you lift both with your eyes closed.

Obviously, this illusion is worthy of deep and weighty consideration.

THE INCREDIBLE SHRINKING CUBE

Hold a sugar cube in your hand, close your eyes, and the sugar cube suddenly feels smaller.

You'll need a magnifying glass, a handkerchief, and a sugar cube, die, or other small cube. Hold the cube with the handkerchief covering your hand. (The handkerchief prevents you from seeing your hand, which is itself a clue to the size of things.) Feel the cube through the cloth while looking at it under the magnifying glass for several minutes. Then close your eyes and just feel the cube. Incredibly, it shrinks!

Vision is our dominant sense. When we get conflicting information from touch and vision, we perceive what we see, not what we feel. A cube through a magnifying glass looks larger than it really is, and you feel it as the size you *see* it. When you remove vision and only receive information through touch, you perceive the size of the cube as it really is.

————WHAT'S THE POINT?————

You feel as if your back is being poked with one point when it's really being poked with two. Here's the procedure to fool yourself. Get a large hairpin or open a paper clip to form a V. Have the points an inch apart. Close your eyes and press both points against the back of your hand. Do you feel one point or two? Now press both points against your back. It will feel as if only one point is sticking you.

This phenomenon can be investigated systematically. Do it with a friend—one of you is the subject and the other is the experimenter. The experimenter touches sometimes one point and sometimes two to different parts of the subject's body. The subject is blindfolded and must state whether he or she feels one or two points. Vary the distance between points. You'll find that different parts of the body are more or less sensitive in accurately determining if the stimulus is made up of one or two points. One study showed that the middle finger was the most sensitive. It felt two points as two separate points when they were only 2.5 millimeters apart. The calf was the least sensitive. Two distinct separate points were first felt when they were 47 millimeters or about 2½ inches apart.

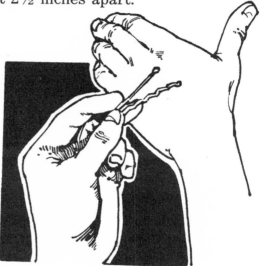

Recently a device has been invented for blind people that transforms an object they would be looking at if they could see into a pattern of pressure points on their back. A lot of practice is needed to learn to identify items correctly. How do your results show why this is so?

——COLD REALITY . . . OR HOT?——

Both your hands are in the same pot of water, which is at room temperature. Yet the water feels cool to one hand and warm to the other. If someone asked you if this water was warm or cool, you would be at a loss for an answer. It's both. How can that be?

Get three large bowls or pots. Fill one with water that is about room temperature. Put ice water in another pot and hot water (as hot as you can comfortably stand it) in the third. Hold one hand in the hot water and the other in the ice water for thirty seconds. Then plunge both hands into the water that is room temperature. The tepid water will feel warm to the hand that's been in ice water and cool to the hand that was in hot water. So your sensation depends on where each hand is coming from.

This illusion was the basis for an extended discussion on the subject of reality by the famous French mathematician and philosopher René Descartes (1596–1650). He concluded from this experiment and other observations that trusting your senses was *not* the way to know reality. True reality came only from ideas, including the idea of doubting one's senses. That's why he said, "I think, therefore I am." His awareness of himself defined existence and reality.

————HERE'S WHAT'S WET————

Your hands are dry, yet they feel wet. To get this weird feeling put rubber gloves on your hands and plunge them into cold water. If you didn't know you had gloves on, you'd swear your hands were wet. Now try warm water. The feeling is not so pronounced. The sensation of "wetness," according to scientists, has two components. One is coldness, and the other is pressure evenly distributed over an area of skin.

The skin is one of the most sensitive and reliable information-gathering organs we have. Correct judgments are often made on the basis of

feel alone. We correctly identify properties such as hardness, softness, smoothness, roughness, stickiness, greasiness, wetness, and dryness. Sci-

entists have tried to figure out the parts of each special feeling with very little success up to now. They suggest that many of these sensations are the result of "touch blends." Theoretically, if you have broken down the components of a touch blend, you should be able to simulate it by putting them back together without using the real thing. Thus cold water perceived through a rubber glove makes you feel as if you have wet hands even when they're dry.

Here are some analyses of other skin "feelings." See if you can think up ways to create these feelings artifically.

1. Hardness—even, cold pressure with a distinct boundary.
2. Softness—uneven, warm pressure with no distinct boundary.
3. Stickiness—uneven, moving, jerky pressure.

This is one area that's wide open for ground-breaking discoveries. So dig in!

————A SENSE OF HORROR————

Want to try some really spooky sensations? Here's where you feel perfectly ordinary objects to which your learned expectations can add a dimension of horror. Close your eyes, add a little

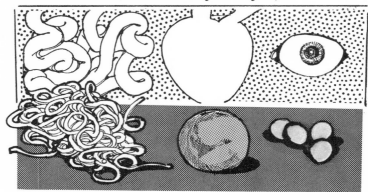

imagination, and feel eyeballs, brains, and a cold, dead heart. These illusions are the stuff of Halloween and haunted houses. Think grim and macabre thoughts while you close your eyes and feel the following foods: cold, wet grapes are great eyeballs; cold, wet macaroni feels like brains might feel. Plunge a whole tomato into boiling water for about twenty seconds. Then peel off the skin. Chill in the refrigerator. Hold the cold, peeled tomato and imagine that it's a heart.

Share these weird and horrible sensations with your friends. The common quality of all these materials is *clamminess*. Scientists have described clamminess as "a cold softness felt with movement and accompanied by unpleasant mental pictures." Some scientists believe that the emotions of anxiety, love, and disgust are simply skin sensations (as if they were simple!) along with changes in internal chemistry. Perhaps deep feeling is not so deep after all. Love, along with horror, may be only skin deep.

——HOW TO KEEP FROM KIDDING—— ——YOURSELF——

How well do you know yourself? You may have secret desires that you are not aware of.

Maybe you *are* fooling yourself and don't know it. Here's a stunt that tells you what you *really*

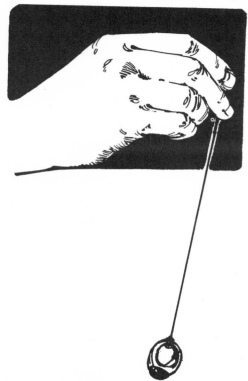

think. Maybe. You'll need to make a pendulum by tying a weight on the end of a ten-inch string.

Let the weight hang freely. Hold the end of the string as steady as possible. A circular motion by the pendulum bob means "yes" and a back-and-forth motion means "no." Start asking yourself questions and observe the motion of

the bob. Some questions might be: "Do I really like———?" "Do I want———to happen?" Then try some questions where the answer is obvious just to see how accurate the pendulum swings are: "Is my name———?" and see if you get a "yes." You may be surprised at the accuracy of the pendulum.

Here's an idea explaining this one. Everyone has muscle tension that is too small to detect easily. Such tension is called "covert" because it is covered or hidden. The motion of the pendulum magnifies tiny muscular movements, thus revealing covert muscular responses to the questions you ask yourself.

Try this one out on friends. Make sure that they try to hold the pendulum as steadily as possible. Give each answer time to develop.

———NO SIGN OF A SIGNATURE———

You think you can write your name automatically and without effort, right? Wrong. Here's a way to completely destroy your ability to sign your name.

Sit at a table with a pencil and paper. Depending on whether you are right- or left-handed, use your favored foot to trace circles on the floor. Once you get your foot going, watch it to make certain it keeps moving in a circle. Now try to sign your name. The scrawl you produce will

make you feel helpless. If you do succeed in signing your name fairly legibly, chances are that

your foot has traced similar motions. You have not kept it moving in a circle.

The muscle-coordination problem here is similar to rubbing your stomach and patting your head at the same time. With practice it is possible to master this one. Some weird people may think it's worth the effort.

────── A WHIRLING WORLD ──────

Want to feel the earth move even with your feet planted firmly on the ground? All you have

to do is destroy your sense of balance. Dizziness makes you feel as if the world is whirling about you although it is as steady as ever, and an expert on vertigo told us that the following method for producing dizziness is the zonker of all times.

Hold a baseball bat, handle up, on the floor. Put your forehead on the base of the handle. Walk around the bat three times. Now stand up and tell yourself that the earth is not moving. That should do it.

Your sense of balance is controlled by three tubelike canals in each of your inner ears. Dizziness is caused when the fluid in these canals is set in motion. Spinning around with your head up will set this fluid in motion in one direction. But when you place your head in another position and then turn around, you create all kinds of unusual motion that makes everything seem to tilt and spin. It's a good thing the effect is temporary!

Strange Sounds
and
a Taste for the Mysterious

People who become lost in the woods have been
known to wander about in large circles thinking
that they are walking in a straight line. They
have the illusion that their sense of direction is

accurate. The reality is that hearing is a far more reliable sense for finding your way out of such circumstances than a "sense of direction." Hearing is important for perceiving distance and direction. The best way to find civilization is to walk toward a sound, such as a brook or highway. You know when you are getting nearer because the sound gets louder.

Our ears are amazing devices for detecting an enormous variety of sounds. Inside our ears are thin, sensitive membranes—eardrums—that respond to sound. Sound is created by vibrating air that presses against our eardrums, setting them in motion. The motion of our eardrums is then translated to nerve impulses to the brain through a complex series of events. The range of the ear's sensitivity is enormous. We hear the simplest sounds, such as tones from a tuning fork, including high ones and low ones. We enjoy the complexities of the organized sound of music and the subtle differences in voices. Our brain focuses attention on different kinds of sound. We can pick up the soft sound of a pin dropping, when we pay attention, and yet tune out loud background noise that would interfere with concentration.

There are relatively few hearing illusions as compared with visual illusions. Much of the time we are fooled by the ways we interpret sounds.

If you are alone at night, you may hear all kinds of spooky sounds. More often than not, it's your imagination (your brain, not your ears) working overtime.

Your chemical senses of taste and smell can also be fooled. The receptors for taste are located in bumps, called taste buds, on your tongue, along your throat, and on the roof of your mouth. They fire when molecules from food in your saliva come in contact with them. The receptors for smell are found in the lining of the upper part of the cavity inside the nose. They also fire when molecules come in contact with them.

Smell is remarkable for two reasons. First, it is extremely sensitive. Some scientists estimate that smell is 10,000 times more sensitive than taste. It responds to extremely small numbers of molecules. Second, smell is the fastest-adapting of all our senses. You've noticed this when you come across a strong and unpleasant odor. Within a few minutes you'll adapt and no longer notice the smell.

Smell and taste are very closely associated. Without smell you would have very little appreciation for fine cooking. Taste would be limited to the basic flavors which are sweet, salty, bitter, and sour. Remove smell, and you can be fooled by taste alone. The taste of foods is also affected by the sense of touch. The texture and temperature of foods—the way food feels in your mouth—is also a part of your perception and can be part of an illusion.

Illusions of hearing and the chemical senses are fascinating, but there are not too many of them compared to vision. For this reason, we're putting them in one chapter. Hear and taste the unreal.

—HEAR A SOUND AND KNOW NOT— ——————WHERE——————

This is an illusion where you cannot locate sounds. You can't tell if the sound is in front of you, behind you, above you, or to either side of you. Sit blindfolded on a stool in the middle of a room. The only rule is that you may not move your head at all. You will need three friends, each with a clicker such as you can buy in a dime store. One will make a sound above your head, one behind you, and one in front of you. If the sound comes from an imaginary line that is exactly the same distance to each ear, you will not be able to tell where the sound is coming from.

Sound localization depends on sound reaching each ear at slightly different times. This occurs because the distance to a sound is slightly differ-

ent for each ear. Thus a sound takes a fraction of a second longer to reach one ear than the other. This time lag determines the direction from which you hear a sound. When a sound is the same distance from both ears, reaching both ears at the same instant, you will not be able to locate it. Turning your head or cocking it creates unequal distances between your ears and the sound source, helping you find its direction.

Vision can also confuse your ability to locate

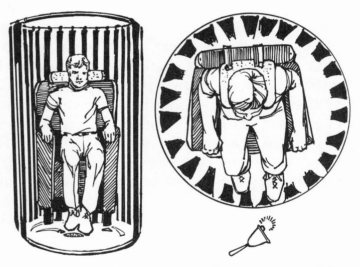

sounds. There is a study that demonstrates this. The person who was the subject in the study was seated on a stool, feet off the ground, with his head held in a brace so that it couldn't be moved. He was surrounded by a shower curtain that had vertical stripes. The shower curtain rotated so that the stripes passed in front of his eyes. A sound made directly in front of the face, but behind the moving curtain, seemed to be coming from directly overhead.

The moving curtain created the illusion of motion (see p. 83). Vertical stripes passing in front of the eyes make you feel as if you are moving along, in a direction opposite to the motion of the stripes. The moving stripes make you feel as if you are moving past the point you are facing.

Past experience teaches that sound changes with motion. Sounds, such as a siren or train whistle, always change in pitch as you pass them or they pass you. If you have a visual illusion of motion, you *know* a sound you appear to be passing *cannot* remain unchanged. So you resolve the conflict by perceiving the sound that's actually in front of you as if it is coming from directly above.

———SOUNDS OF THE SEA———

Hear the ocean roar in your own room far from the sea. Listen to a seashell, or, if you haven't one handy, put your ear against a jar. The sound of the surf crashing against the shore is loud and clear.

But it is only an illusion, noise from your environment, including noise made by your ear brushing against the edge of the shell. These sounds are reinforced by the vibration of the air within the shell or jar. This enhanced sound, called *resonance*, seems very much like the distant roar of the ocean.

SOUND EFFECTS

Sound illusions have a history in radio and the theater. They have long been used to create atmosphere or an event. They depend almost entirely on the listener's past experience. Here is a list of ways to simulate environmental sounds.

Experiment with them. Some require electronic equipment. If you have a microphone and speaker, you can experiment with direct amplification. Do the sound effects directly into the mike. Or, if you have a tape recorder, tape your sound effects and then play them back. If no electronic equipment is available, close your eyes and imagine that you're hearing the real thing!

Rain—Take your choice: put about ¼ cup dried peas in a metal pie pan. Gently move the peas around the pan with a circular motion. Pour sand or rice against a Ping-Pong ball. Make a chute of waxed paper and pour a trickle of sugar along it from the top so that it runs down the chute.

Wind—Pull a silk (or polyester) scarf across two or three strips of wood laid side by side.

For wind in the trees shake some old recording tape near the microphone.

Thunder—Breathe gently on the microphone. Shake a flexible cookie sheet from one corner.

Ocean Waves—Put an assortment of dried peas or rice and some gravel in a vinyl suitcase. Close the case. Rhythmically lift each end so that the contents swish along the case and crash at the end.

Fire—Crumple a large piece of cellophane in front of the microphone.

Foghorn—Blow across a soda bottle. You can vary the pitch with the amount of water in the bottle. (Combine this one with the waves and you'll feel as if you're at sea.)

Gunshot—Whack a ruler against the back of a leather chair or against a wood surface.

Machine Gun—Drum rapidly with an irregular beat with two pencils on the bottom of an empty oatmeal box.

Explosion—Burst a paper bag while recording at the fastest speed your recorder is capable of and play it back at the slowest speed.

Waterfall—Record water running from your faucet at a high speed and play it back at a slow one.

Train—Rhythmically rub two sandpaper blocks together, slowly picking up speed.

Hoofbeats—This is a classic effect. It takes

a bit of practice to get the rhythm right, but the source is two coconut shells (small wooden salad bowls also work). The horse sounds as if he's running on pavement if you drum the shells against the bathroom floor. If you drum against a padded surface, the horse sounds as if he's running on grass.

Jet Plane—Use a hairdryer and make the engines howl by covering the exhaust.

Footsteps in the Snow—Fill a small plastic bag with flour. Rhythmically strike it against a hard surface.

A Voice on the Telephone—Speak into a small plastic cup.

———HOW TO KEEP A SECRET———

A friend who is setting next to you whispers a secret. You think you'll hear it but you don't. You only get the message when the whisperer is facing you. You don't get the message because the whisperer's back is to you.

We tried this indoors with poor results. We could hear whispers quite clearly regardless of which way the whisperer faced. Then we tried it outdoors and it worked! A whisper made facing away from you is impossible to understand even if it is spoken as loud as a normal speaking voice.

The explanation lies in the nature of sound. Sound travels in waves that bend around objects much as water waves bend around small objects on their surface. Sound waves of the low tones of a normal speaking voice bend easily around the speaker's head. That's why you can hear what's said when the speaker faces away from you. Sound waves from a whisper are not as easily bent. They don't travel around the speaker so that they can be heard as words in a message. Sounds of whispers do, however, bounce off walls. That's why this experiment didn't work inside. In fact, the way whispers bounce off walls (it is different from speaking-voice echoes), creates another illusion in whispering galleries. A person can whisper in one part of the gallery and someone on the other side hears it as if it is coming from another place. There a secret can be told across a room although the person receiving the message is nowhere near the teller.

—HOW NOT TO KEEP A SECRET—

If you think a message passed along by ten people or more is going to be the same as it started, forget it. Hearsay evidence is not admissible in a court of law because it is likely to be inaccurate. You can put this to a test.

Gather as many friends as you can—at least ten. Stand or sit them in a line. Whisper a message to the first and request he pass it on by whispering it to the next. Just to make sure you remember exactly what you said, write it down. Make it a simple statement. After the words have been "processed" by each member of the group, have the last person report the message and compare it with the one you have written. The odds are high that they will not be the same. This phenomenon is the basis for the game "Rumor."

People hear selectively. They pay attention to what is familiar to them, and they substitute new words (or omit one or two) according to their own understanding of a message. The difference between the original message and the final result is not a single perceptual illusion. It is the sum of each person's misperception. If there's any lesson to be learned here, it is that you and your friends are not a recording machine.

————WHAT'S THAT AGAIN?————

Did you ever learn to recite something as a young child, only to learn years later that you were saying the wrong thing? One day we read what we have been saying and realize our misconceptions. We've been repeating a mistake for

years and didn't know it! Read the following misstatements aloud. The errors are funny, but understandable.

"*I led the pigeons* to the flag . . . " (I pledge allegiance to the flag . . .)

". . . and to the republic for *Richie Stans* . . ." (. . . and to the republic for which it stands . . .)

". . . one *naked individual* . . ." (. . . one nation indivisible . . .)

"Our Father, who art in heaven, *Harold* be thy name . . ." (hallowed be thy name . . .)

". . . and lead us not into *Penn Station* . . ." (temptation)

"*Shirley, good Mrs. Murphy* shall follow me all of the days of my life . . ." (Surely goodness and mercy . . .)

Neck store neighbor or *next store* neighbor (next-door neighbor)

"The Star-Spangled Banana" or "The Stars-Bangled Banger" ("The Star-Spangled Banner")

The master of words that sound like English was Lewis Carroll, who wrote the poem "Jabberwocky" in *Alice through the Looking Glass*. Here's the first verse that sounds really meaningful with the proper inflections:

> Twas brillig and the slithy toves
> Did gyre and gimble in the wabe:

All mimsy were the borogroves,
And the mome raths outgrabe.

–AN ILLUSION WORTH REPEATING–

You may think you can repeat a simple word aloud and it will stay the same word no matter how many times you say it. But it won't. Say the word "say" over and over again rapidly. At some point it will become the word "ace." It will stay "ace" for a while and then shift abruptly back to "say."

Scientists call this phenomenon "verbal alternation." It is similar to the shifting perception of ambiguous visual forms like the Necker cube on page 59. There are many words that will alternate if you repeat them aloud rapidly. Try the word "rest." It will become "tress" and may become "Esther." You have no control over the alternating form the word takes. You are unconsciously reorganizing certain speech sounds to produce different words.

──WOOD YOU COULD TASTE──

Wood, a substance that's tasteless, acquires a flavor in this illusion. Use the handle of a wooden spoon (the bowl of the spoon may have

taken on the taste of sauces it has stirred), the back end of a wooden matchstick or an ice-cream stick, or a doctor's tongue depressor. Press the wooden stimulator to different parts of the tongue—the tip, the sides, the back. See if the wood takes on one of the four basic tastes—sweet, sour, salty, or bitter—depending on where you touch it.

As stated previously, taste receptors are located in the bumps on your tongue called taste buds. Different taste buds are responsible for the different basic tastes. Although taste buds for all four tastes are located all over the tongue, there are more sweet receptors on the tip, more sour on the sides, and more bitter at the back. Salt receptors seem more evenly distributed than the others.

Our source for this illusion claims that the mechanical stimulation by a tasteless object fires the receptors, making it appear to have a taste. We tried this and got different results with different people. Some people were more sensitive than others.

————FLAVORLESS COFFEE————

The distinctive flavor of coffee can be almost completely eliminated, leaving only a bitter taste in your mouth. This experiment shows how important your sense of smell is for experiencing full flavors.

Hold your nose and put a few grains of fresh coffee grounds in your mouth. Chew them. Now open your nose. Suddenly the characteristic flavor of coffee fills your mouth. Now you know why preparing gourmet food for someone with a cold is wasted effort. Receptors in your nose respond to all kinds of molecules your taste buds are incapable of responding to.

NAME THAT FOOD

Here's how you can be prevented from being able to tell the difference between an apple, a raw potato, or an onion. Put on a blindfold and nose clips. (You can hold your nose, if you keep

it air tight.) Have a friend place a small piece of one of the above three foods on your tongue. Guess what it is just from the taste without chewing. (The texture is a clue that can give it away.) You will make mistakes because, again, it's largely differences in their odors which make them taste different.

You can also check your sense of taste when

it comes to telling the difference between Coke and 7-Up. A blindfold and nose clips make it almost impossible. The beverages taste surprisingly alike. They are both lemon-lime based drinks although one is sweeter than the other. You'll have no problem telling the difference with your senses of smell and vision operating.

————FALSE SWEETNESS————

Here are two ways to make water taste sweet without putting anything sweet into it. Salt makes your tastebuds especially sensitive to other tastes. Shake some salt on one side of your tongue. Give it a minute to become sensitive to the taste. Now put water on the other side of your tongue. (Use a spoon to dribble it over the surface.) How does the water taste? We found it was definitely sweet. If the water is slightly sweetened, it will now taste very sweet. People salt melons and grapefruit because a little salt makes them taste sweeter.

Artichokes contain a chemical that alters the receptors on your tongue so that water or milk will taste sweet. Wash a fresh artichoke by running water through it and turning it upside down to drain. Put it in a saucepan with water halfway up its sides and boil it, covered, until the center

feels tender when you stick a fork into it. Remove the leaves to expose the heart. Cut off the bristle-

like choke. Chew a quarter of the heart and hold it in your mouth for one minute. Now drink some water or milk. It will have a sweet flavor. (You'll find the same effect from eating the leaves.) Chemists are trying to isolate the chemical in artichokes that produces this effect for use as an artificial sweetener. Fine chefs do not like to serve vintage wines with artichokes because the true flavor of the wine cannot be appreciated by an artichoke-doctored tongue.

—FOOD THAT'S ALMOST THE REAL—
—————THING—————

There are a number of qualities that are part of the distinctive tastes of different foods. These include flavor, temperature, and texture. Vegetarian cooks often try to create meatlike dishes without using meat. We've given you two recipes for fake meat. There is a slight difference between these fakes and the real thing. But one of our tasters who doesn't like chopped liver, didn't like these substitutes either. And we bet your tasters will have a hard time figuring out what these dishes are really made from, especially the last one, a cracker pie.

Fake Chopped Liver
½ cup chopped celery
1 chopped onion
¼ cup oil
5 hard-boiled eggs
4 ounces chopped walnuts
  salt, pepper, garlic powder to taste

1. Brown the celery and onions in the oil.
2. Chop or grind browned celery and onions, eggs, and walnuts in a wooden chopping bowl, food processor, or meat grinder.

3. Season with salt, pepper, and garlic powder. Serve chilled on crackers on a bed of lettuce with a slice of tomato.

Fake Hamburgers
½ pound lentils
1 tbs. butter
1 small onion, chopped
½ cup rough vegetable protein (can be purchased at any health-food store)
2 eggs
salt, pepper, garlic powder to taste
cracker meal
cooking oil or margarine

1. Simmer lentils in a partly covered saucepan with enough water to cover over a low flame for one hour. Drain well and place in a large mixing bowl.
2. Brown the chopped onion in butter. Add to the lentils.
3. Add rough vegetable protein, raw eggs, and seasoning. Mix well with your hands.
4. Form into patties and coat with cracker meal by placing each patty on some meal in a dish.
5. Heat the oil or margarine in a skillet until hot. Cook the patties about five minutes on each side. Serve hot with catsup. A ham-

burger roll and a slice of raw onion add to the illusion.

Mock Apple Pie

This is a humdinger of an illusion. No one will believe that this pie is not made of apples but RITZ Crackers. Here's the recipe right off a Nabisco RITZ Crackers box:

Pastry for two crust 9-inch pie
36 RITZ crackers
 2 cups water
 2 cups sugar
 2 tsp. cream of tartar
 2 tbs. lemon juice
grated rind of one lemon
butter or margarine
cinnamon

Roll out bottom crust of pastry and fit into 9-inch pie plate. Break RITZ Crackers coarsely into the pastry-lined plate. Combine the water, sugar, and cream of tartar in a saucepan; boil gently for 15 minutes. Add lemon juice and rind. Cool. Pour the syrup over the crackers, dot the crackers generously with butter or margarine, and sprinkle with cinnamon. Cover with the top crust. Trim and flute the edges by pressing all around with a fork. Cut slits with a sharp knife

on the top crust to let the steam escape. Bake
in a hot oven (425° F) 30 to 35 minutes until crust
is crisp and golden. Serve warm. Cut into 6 or
8 slices.

Bizarre Shapes and Sizes

Your sense of sight depends on the light from objects you look at forming an image on the light-sensitive area on the back of the eyeball called the *retina*. The size of an image on your retina

depends in part on the distance the object is from your eye. When someone walks away from you, his image on your retina gets smaller. That is a fact. It is also a fact that within limits you are not aware of this change in size. A person six feet tall still appears to be six feet tall despite their shrinking image. You interpret this change in the size of the image as a change in distance. Your view of such a shrinking image as moving away from you while remaining the same size is called *size constancy.* Size constancy enables artists to create an illusion of depth in a flat picture. The skillful use of the angles of lines and the sizes of objects in a painting gives it depth or "perception." Nearby objects are made larger than those supposed to be distant. A skillful artist can make a flat surface appear three-dimensional. In these pictures the distant figure looks "normal." When it is moved to the foreground it seems surprisingly small.

Suggestions of depth in simple line figures are the basis of many of the classic optical illusions in this chapter. Other illusions included here are caused by the way we judge length. Vertical figures look longer than horizontal ones although they may be exactly the same. Still another kind of illusion is based on the brain and the eyes getting conflicting information. When you look at some of these apparently simple figures, their form changes back and forth as if your brain can't quite make up its mind about what you are seeing. This last sentence is a good example of one that gives no information about why we see what we see. ". . . A brain that can't make up its mind . . ." *profoundly* reveals how little we know about what's really happening.

Enjoy your confusion as you view these illusions.

SIMPLE CHALLENGES TO THE EYE

There are a number of illusions that have been known to psychologists for about a hundred years. Their significance is that they seem to be the simplest of illusions around—a few lines, angles, and shapes, and we're down to the bare basics of deception. Many of them are named for the scientists who discovered them.

Which line of the Müller-Lyer figure is longer?

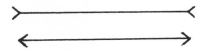

Measure them. The two vertical lines are the same length. Psychologists state that the infor-

mation for the length of a line is not simply its length. The angles of the superimposed lines at the ends somehow affect our judgment. Which shape in this Wundt illusion is larger?

The two shapes are the same size. The upper figure appears smaller because its shorter arc is next to the longer arc of the lower figure. The position makes the upper figure seem smaller.

All the long lines in the next two figures are parallel. They appear to bulge in the Hering illusion, and cave in in the Wundt illusion.

You can see how these lines are parallel by holding the book up to one eye, closing the other eye, and looking down the lines. The superimposed lines will be too indistinct to be the distraction necessary for the illusion.

Artists create the illusion of depth in pictures. They draw what appear to be parallel lines, like railroad tracks, at angles to meet at some point.

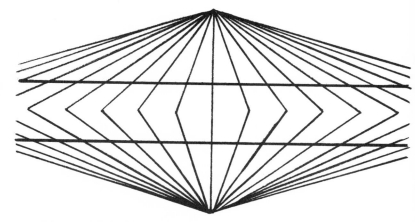

This point appears to be in the distance. It is called the vanishing point.

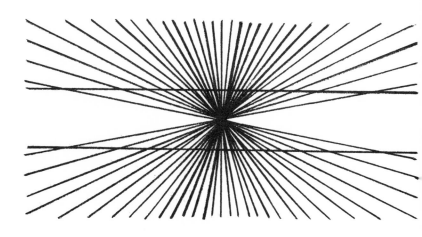

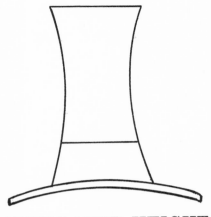

—————OVERRATED HEIGHT—————

You may think that this tophat is taller than the width of the brim. If so, you're wrong.

One of our common failings is that we perceive height as greater than width even when they are the same. This is called the vertical-horizontal illusion. A tree that is standing is estimated as being taller than when it is lying on the ground. You can experiment with this when you shop for a Christmas tree.

Here's another way to show you how far off your sense of vertical distance is from your sense of horizontal. Make a dot with a black pen on a sheet of white paper. Make a second dot about one inch directly above it. Now make a third dot along an imaginary line at right angles to an imaginary line between the first two dots so that this third dot appears to be the same distance away. Measure your efforts. How good is your eye at estimating equal distances horizontally and vertically?

One explanation for this misperception is that it takes more effort to raise our eyes up and down to judge height than from side to side to judge width. As a result, we tend to judge height as greater because of the greater effort involved in viewing it.

————ALTERNATING FORMS————

Study this figure for a while. Do you see a white vase or two black profiles?

Is this "book" opening toward you or away from you?

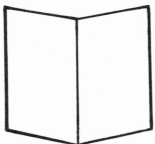

This figure is called the "Necker Cube" after the man who first drew it. Which corner is nearest to you?

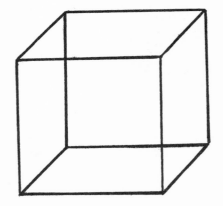

These are three examples of what are called reversible ambiguous figures. All the distance, direction, and contrast cues are equal. As a result, your brain cannot decide what it is looking at, so you see alternate forms that switch back and forth. Sometimes you see the vase, sometimes the profiles; sometimes one corner seems closer, and sometimes another. You can have some conscious control as to which form you see, but after a while the figure will spontaneously switch back or "reverse" to the alternate form. It is part of our Western culture to be uncomfortable with ambiguity and to regard a figure as more important than the background. Many of us find that looking at these figures is not a pleas-

ant experience. Oriental cultures differ in their perception of such figures. Eastern cultures accept uncertainty and ambiguity. The Yin/Yang symbol expresses the idea that the figure and background are meaningless without each other. It would be interesting to see if someone brought up in China or Japan has the same discomfort in viewing these ambiguous figures that you have.

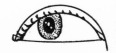

IMPOSSIBLE PICTURES

A paradox is the result of two sets of information from the same source that cannot exist together. An artist can put together the clues for depth in a drawing to create a figure that cannot possibly exist in three dimensions. Artist Maurice Escher's works are famous for their visual paradoxes. When we look at these pictures, we find it disturbing that we cannot construct a mental picture of the "real" object.

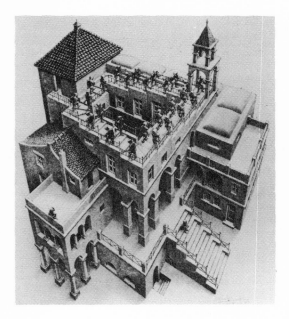

Which is the bottom step of this staircase?

This drawing is called a blivit. Where is the middle prong attached?

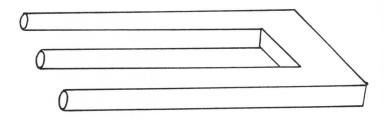

Which angle of this triangle is closest to you?

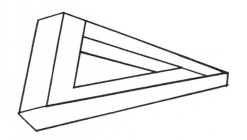

When you look at separate parts of each of these figures they appear possible. You run into trouble when you try to figure out how the whole thing is put together.

—A PENNY FOR YOUR THOUGHTS—

Can you fit a penny on this drawing of a table so that it doesn't touch any of the lines? It certainly appears large enough. Try it.

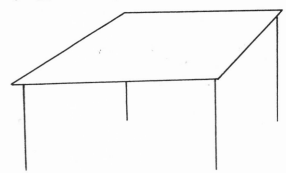

The angles of the table top give it an illusion of depth that makes it seem larger than it really is. The actual geometric shape is smaller than the penny. Would you be fooled if there were no legs on the table? Or does it make no difference?

A full moon looks much larger when it is just rising than later on in the night when it is high in the sky. Its *apparent* size has been measured as 1.2 to 1.5 times larger on the horizon than at its zenith. This is one of the classic illusions of all time. If you photograph the moon on the horizon and then high in the sky from the same location and measure the diameters, they will be the same.

The enlarged size of the moon is related to seeing the moon close to familiar distance cues over the horizon. These cues are not available when it is high in the sky. Look at the moon on the horizon through a tiny window made by the thumbs and forefingers of both hands held up to your eye, blocking out everything but the moon. It immediately appears smaller.

STRAIGHTENING OUT YOUR MIND'S ——————————EYE———————————

Is one slanted line in this figure a continuation of the other? If they look as if they are not contin-

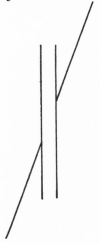

uous, you are seeing the Poggendorf illusion. Poggendorf discovered that when a slanted line is interrupted by two parallel lines, its separated halves look as if they wouldn't meet each other.

There is a complicated explanation for this illusion that has to do with the way we estimate angles. If the crossing line is at right angles to the parallel lines, we have no trouble seeing that they meet. As the angle changes from 90°, we have increasing problems seeing that they meet.

You can, however, straighten yourself out. Imagine a hand pulling at each end of the slanted lines as if they were having a tug of war with a rope. As the tension increases, watch as the rope straightens out across the gap.

————THE AMES WINDOW————

This one you have to see to believe! A window you know to be rotating appears to be waving back and forth. A pencil stuck through one of the openings seems to bend around the window. This illusion involves a fairly elaborate setup and some experimentation, but the results are well worth it.

Trace or make two photocopies of the trapezoid window drawn here. Cut them out and trace the

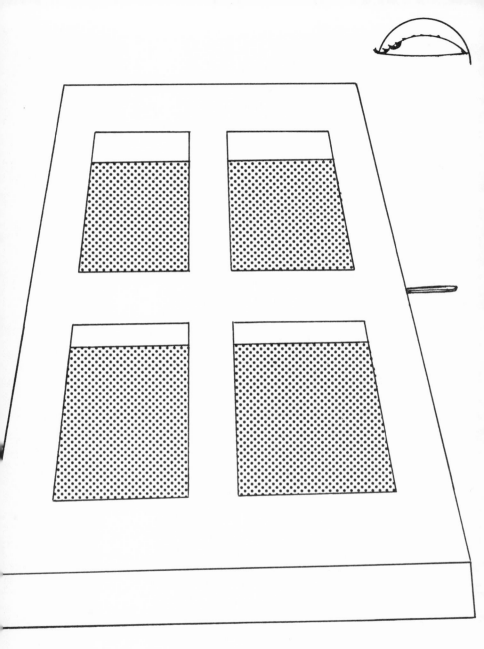

shape on a piece of cardboard. Cut out the cardboard and paste a trapezoid on each side. Cut
out the openings. Mount the window on a long
toothpick at the balance points by sticking it between the paper and cardboard. The toothpick
will hold its position if you use enough paste.
Make a stand for the "window" by sticking the
end of the toothpick into a salt shaker.

The illusion is created by slowly and steadily
rotating the window on a turntable. One of our
sources recommended two revolutions per minute. A phonograph turntable at 33 rpm is much

too fast. We used a lazy Susan turned by hand. Put the salt shaker on the turntable so that the toothpick is over the center. Have a friend turn the table while you observe it in dim light from a distance of about ten feet with one eye covered. A plain background, like a white wall surface, helps.

There are some variations you can check out. Observe the window in the dark by illuminating it with a flashlight. The shadow will also appear to be waving back and forth instead of rotating. Stick a pencil through one opening and tape it in place or put a red dot on one side of the small end of the trapezoid. The effect is so dramatic we can't really give its effect in words.

This illusion is caused by a conflict created by the shape of the window. The narrow end makes the window look as if it is a rectangle pointing away from you. Converging lines are a distance cue for parallel lines. You saw this in the railroad tracks. When this smaller end moves toward you, your brain still perceives it as if it were at the far end. You see the window moving away from you even when it is moving toward you.

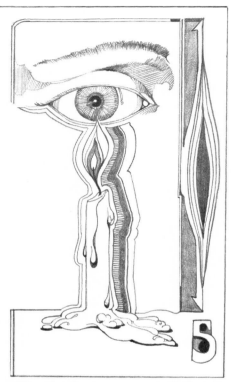

Brightness Mad
and
Color Crazed

Your eyes have two kinds of vision depending on how much light reaches them. You've noticed this difference when you've entered a dark theater on a bright day. For the first few minutes

you can't see much of anything. This is the first period of what scientists call "dark adaptation," a process that has two distinct stages. The first stage is the rapid change that is completed after about seven minutes. At the end of this period you can see your way around the theater, but your vision is not very sharp. The second stage of dark adaptation begins after twelve minutes, and you'll notice that you are able to see an increasing amount of detail. After forty-five minutes, you'll be seeing about as well as you possibly can in dim light, although some scientists claim that slow improvement continues for up to twenty-four hours.

The adjustment to bright light, on the other hand, is very rapid. Your eyes may hurt, and you'll be temporarily blinded when you reenter the street after being in the theater. But the adjustment is complete within two minutes.

The double-adaptation process is due to two kinds of receptors in the eye. The center of the retina contains receptors called cone cells, which are sensitive to bright light and to colors. Night vision is the work of receptors called rod cells, which are found surrounding the central area. There is some overlap between the sensitivity of rods and cones that makes you susceptible to illusions at low illuminations. Also, the contrast between bright areas and dark areas is often confusing. Bright areas are seen as larger than dark. Light-colored shapes seem larger than dark-colored shapes. The French discovered this illusion when they designed their three-colored flag. Originally the flag had three vertical stripes of equal width: one blue, one white, and one red. But the blue stripe looked wider than the red one. So the flag was redesigned in the proportions of 30, 33, and 37. Now the stripes look equal. (See the differences in the illustration on the cover of this book.)

Colors also appear different, depending on what is next to them. The cover of this book has a red patch next to a purple patch next to a blue patch. The purple patch doesn't appear to be uniform in color. It looks bluish next to the red patch and reddish near the blue patch. Cover the red and blue patches, and you'll see the purple patch as uniform. Artists make use of the effect of one color on the other to create illusions of size and distance.

The illusions in this chapter are based on the strange things that happen in what you might consider the twilight zone.

—THE CASE OF THE BULGING——
———————BORDERS———————

Which circle looks larger, the white or the black?

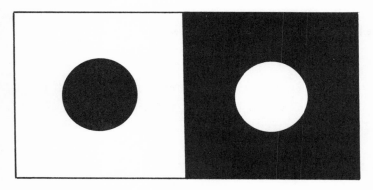

Would you believe they're the same size? (Of course you would, given your experience in reading this book.) In general, bright objects look larger than dark objects. Here's an example from nature. A crescent moon is the brightly illuminated rim of a sphere. Most of the illuminated surface faces away from us. If you look carefully, however, you can see the rest of the sphere due to reflected light from the earth, or earth shine. The arms of the crescent moon seem swollen larger than the dark part of the sphere, giving rise to an old saying that there is "a new moon with the old moon in its arms."

Here are some other examples: The filament

of a light bulb appears to swell when it glows. If you hold a pencil in front of a candle flame, the pencil appears narrower in front of the flame due to the apparent bulging of the background. Advertisers design packages in light colors to make them appear larger than they really are. Fashion designers suggest dark colors for fat people to make them seem slimmer than they really are.

One explanation for this is that bright light stimulates the retina to cause a spreading effect. Cells next to the ones that light actually falls on are also stimulated to fire, and so there isn't a clear boundary to the image.

————THE HERMANN GRID————

Look at one of the black squares. Do you see dark spots where the white bars cross?

Now look directly at an intersection between white bars. The ghostly dark spot disappears when you look directly at it, but the "ghosts" in your peripheral vision remain strong.

This illusion depends on two aspects of vision. The first is that white appears to be whiter when it is next to black. The white bars between the black squares appear whiter than at the intersec-

tions. An intersection is seen as white meeting white and thus appears less white than next to black. Ghostly, darker areas are the result.

The second aspect of vision is that the cone receptors respond more accurately to bright light than do rod receptors. Cone cells are located in the center of the retina. When you look directly at the intersection, you clearly see that no dark area exists. The rods in the peripheral field of vision are responsible for the illusion. They demonstrate a phenomenon called inhibition. Receptors that are firing inhibit neighboring receptors from firing, thus producing areas of darkness.

This theory, by the way, is in conflict with the

theory explaining the last illusion. How can receptors stimulate neighboring receptors in one case and inhibit them in another? None of the experts we asked could clear up this problem. Perhaps it will challenge you!

——THE CORNSWEET ILLUSION——

A white whirling disk has two areas of brightness despite even illumination. The difference is caused by the shape of a spur in a pit-shaped cutout. To create this illusion you will need a flat white paper plate about six inches in diameter (we cut out the center of a ten-inch paper plate), scissors, tape, and some kind of rotating motor such as a hand mixer, electric drill, or 78 rpm turntable. Cut out the wedge in the plate as shown in the illustration. Make a central hole slightly smaller than the diameter of the shaft of the mixer beater, drill bit, or central shaft

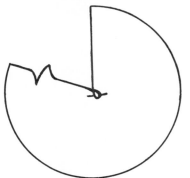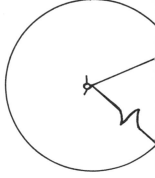

of the turntable. Cut two small slits in the hole as shown. This will make the disk fit snugly around the shaft of the beater or drill bit.

NOTE: There is some danger of getting hurt if an electric drill or hand mixer is not used properly. Ask for adult supervision before you do this experiment.

Put the disk on the shaft. Rotate the motor at different speeds. Although the center of the disk and the outer border are illuminated exactly the same amount, the division caused by the spur in the cutout (disk 1) will make the center seem brighter. If you make a second disk as shown, with the spur reversed, the border will seem brighter.

The white spur of the disk creates a variation that makes the area next to it increase in brightness. The cutout spur creates a local variation that makes the area next to it seem dimmer. If the spurs are covered over with a piece of paper taped over the contours, the inside and outside appear equally bright.

——————MEYER'S EXPERIMENT——————

The result of this experiment is not black or white but a distinct color. That is, you see a color although the color you're looking at is not a color at all but gray cardboard.

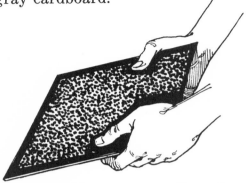

Place a small square of gray cardboard or paper on a bright red or green background. Cover both the square and the background with two or three thicknesses of waxed paper or a single layer of tissue paper. Gaze at the gray square. If the background is red, the square takes on the complementary color of blue-green. If the paper is green, the square appears reddish.

The illusion of color disappears if the gray square is enclosed in a black outline, or if it is placed on top of the waxed paper.

——BENHAM'S TOP AND OTHER—— ——————SPIN-OFFS——————

See colors that aren't there. Color vision is stimulated by a whirling black and white disk

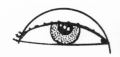

once called Benham's top because it was designed as a child's toy. Copy the black and white pattern illustrated here on a white, 4″ disk. Make the black very black with India ink. Rotate the disk on different devices from a pencil point (if you haven't got anything motorized) to a phonograph turntable to an electric hand mixer. (We

stuck our disks to the beater of an electric hand mixer with a circular loop of tape.)

When you spin the disk (in a strong light) in a clockwise direction, you will see a series of rings ranging from a bluish color on the outside, greenish in the middle, and reddish in the center. Reverse the rotation and the color sequence is also reversed. Try this at various speeds. Different people react differently and see colors at different speeds, so be patient until you see the illusion. If you rotate the disk very fast, the entire thing becomes yellowish. Try rotating the second pattern, which is a variation of the first.

The theory behind this illusion is uncertain. Some scientists feel that the disk causes white light to hit the retina in interrupted flashes, thus stimulating us to "see" colors. Somehow the flashing lights stimulate the retinal receptors to fire.

The illusion conveyed with the third disk is

known as Plateau's spiral. You believe that you are either looking into a tunnel or a tunnel is pushing out at you, depending on the direction of the rotation. At high speeds you don't see the tunneling illusion, but the entire disk takes on a rosy glow. This disk also produces the water-fall illusion discussed in chapter 6.

────THE PURKINJE SHIFT────

You think that you see the colors of the world as they are, red and yellow tulips, green grass, blue bachelor's buttons. But think again. Don't grasses and trees at times seem to be an extra bright green, or perhaps yellow tulips appear to be darker. But have they really changed colors? No. All that's changed is the amount of light—twilight has fallen. This phenomenon, known as the Purkinje shift, is related to the way our eyes function as they slowly adjust from color vision that operates in bright illumination to night vision that operates in dim illumination. Reds and yellows seem brighter to you in daylight and seem less bright than greens and blues at dusk. For this reason greens seem unnaturally bright as the light fades. You may also notice this shift when you look outside during a summer shower.

You can see the Purkinje shift if you study a colored photograph of a landscape in sunlight and then observe it in dim light. The greens in the picture seem to jump out at you. Purkinje (1787–1869), a Bohemian physiologist, discovered this effect in the early nineteenth century. He noticed the change in brightness while looking at an oriental carpet at dusk.

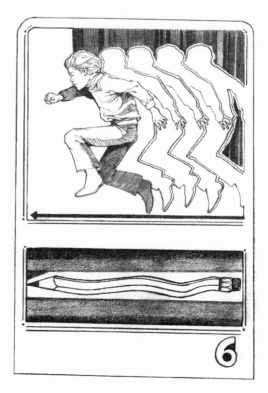

Phantom Moves

The human race could not have survived without recognizing motion. Perceiving moving objects was necessary for us as hunters and as protection from being hunted. We see movement of both prey and enemy as the real movement it is. There is, perhaps, no better demonstration of the accuracy of movement perception than in spurts. Many ball games require split-second responses to moving balls and opponents. Clearly, such motion is part of reality.

But there is a lot of movement we see as motion that is not movement at all. It's called apparent motion. We can also see moving objects as if they are standing still. We misjudge objects we think are moving when these objects are actually motionless. Sometimes we are not sure what direction an object is moving and the speed with which it is moving. We are perhaps more vulnerable to illusions of motion than illusions of contrast, distance, and color.

Some real motion is invisible to us. We cannot see objects moving as fast as a speeding bullet. Our eyes cannot see the motion of objects that move as slowly as the minute hand of a clock. We know it is moving only because we see its position change over a period of time.

In order for us to perceive motion, at least one of three things must happen, although sometimes all three occur at once. First, if an image moves across our retinas, motion is perceived. Our peripheral visual field is especially sensitive. Often we spot something move, say, an object falling outside a window, out of the "corner of

our eye." Second, if we move our eyeballs to keep an image of a moving object in the same place in our visual field, motion is perceived. This activity is called "tracking" and is performed automatically. The final important clue to motion

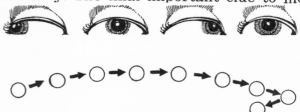

is if we move our head or body to keep an object in sight. There is no doubt in the mind of an observer sitting by the net at a tennis match that the ball is moving. In addition, we all learn how other clues such as changes in size, brightness, and clarity of object indicate motion. For example, we usually interpret a shrinking image as an object that is moving away from us.

The experiments in this chapter will open your eyes to movement that is not real, real motions you cannot see, and a number of other kinds of false moves.

———MOVE FROM A DISPLACED——— ———————EYEBALL———————

You can produce the illusion of a moving object

with your eyeball. Close one eye. Look at an object. Now gently push on the side of your eyeball (on the lid, of course). The object moves around. You don't for one moment believe that the object is actually moving because you feel your eyeball being pushed into a strained position. But there are many times when the movement of your eyeballs is part of the information by which you perceive motion, although you are not consciously aware that they are moving. For example, whenever your eyes follow a ball flying through the air, you perceive real motion. This is in spite of the fact that the image stays in the same place on your retina.

The motion you perceive with your eyes can be transferred to your sense of your whole body moving. You may have noticed this in the movies. If the screen shows a road disappearing in front of the hood of a car viewed through a windshield, and if you concentrate on this and ignore visual clues that you are in a theater, you will feel as if you are moving in the car.

———————OCULAR PARALLAX———————

Want to see a nearby object jump from one place to another without really moving? Look at something that is about a foot and a half in

front of your eyes and alternate opening and closing each eye. If you alternate your eye winks fast enough, the object will appear to dance back and forth in front of you.

The reason for this apparent motion is that your eyes view the object from slightly different positions. The angle of sight makes the object shift slightly compared to its background. With both eyes open, this difference in position is fused into one image and you see depth. (More on this in the next chapter.) When you look with only one eye and then the other, you become aware of the change in position.

In this illusion you know that the object isn't really moving because you are aware of the work your eyes are doing. Parallax is the apparent change in position of an object due to the change in the position of the observer. Ocular parallax means that each eye is in a different position to observe an object relative to its background. The slight change in the position of relatively nearby stars against the pattern of background stars was proof that the earth moves. The shift is due, of course, to the changing position of the viewer on earth as the earth orbits the sun. Parallax is discussed again in chapter 8.

TRAVELING MOON

Look out at the moon through your car window. It is moving so quickly that it's keeping up with you. The moon is traveling with you, or so it seems.

Of course, the moon is *not* moving with you. What you see is an illusion. Nearby objects fly past your moving vehicle. Their position in your line of sight changes rapidly. The moon is so far away that it hardly changes its position relative to your eyes. For this reason, it appears to be moving with you.

The real motion of the moon across the sky, due to the rotation of the earth, is so slow that you don't see it moving. All you see is its position changing over a period of time.

FALSE MOVES

You are sitting in a train looking out of the window. You see the train next to you move and feel as if you are finally starting your journey. It's a surprise to discover that you are not actually moving but that the train next to you is. The clue is a glimpse of the platform, which is stationary.

This illusion is created by viewing a large mov-

ing object that is filling your visual field. The window limits your visual field to only the moving train, which fills it. Your eyes track the train moving next to you as if you were actually moving yourself, thus creating the sensation of whole body motion.

A similar illusion, called the Duncker effect, is created when you observe an enclosed object through a moving framework or environment. A good example is looking at the moon through clouds, where the moon is the enclosed object framed by clouds. The moon appears to be moving through the clouds, although it is the clouds that are actually moving. The tops of tall buildings may also appear to be moving when seen against a background of moving clouds.

——THE WATERFALL ILLUSION——

In 1860 the famous German physiologist and physicist Hermann von Helmholtz (1821–1894) noticed something very peculiar after he had been looking out of the window of a moving train for some time. When he observed the inside of the railroad car, it also appeared to be moving but in a direction opposite to the view of the landscape.

This effect has come to be known as the "waterfall illusion." You can see it if you gaze at an actual waterfall for a while. If you shift your view to the banks on one side, it will appear to be moving upward. If you watch snowflakes falling, tracking them individually as they move down, and then shift your gaze to the ground, the snow on the ground will appear to rise. If a disk with a spiral (see chapter 5) on it is rotated at 33 rpm on a turntable, and you study it under good illumination for a while, you will notice that the figure seems to shrink. When you stop its motion, it will seem to expand in the opposite direction.

This is a kind of afterimage effect. The receptors that perceive motion in one direction get tired. When you stop looking, receptors for motion in the opposite direction are not inhibited from firing. You perceive motion in the opposite direction.

DANCING STAR POINT

Lie on the grass on a starry night and try and stare at a single star. It will dance before your eyes, gliding and wandering about in an unpredictable manner. This phenomenon is called the *autokinetic effect,* meaning "self-motion" because one theory states it is caused by the fact that your eyes are never at rest and are continually moving. Most of the time, you are not aware of this motion.

You can see the autokinetic effect even more dramatically with a simple lab setup. Make a pinhole in a shoe box. Put a lit flashlight in the box and tape the cover down so that it is light tight. Observe the tiny source of light in a per-

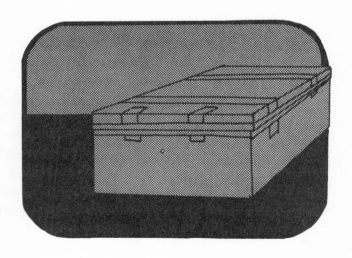

fectly dark room. It is very important that the room be completely dark and that you have given yourself time to adapt to the dark before observing the light source. The point of light will move in very dramatic ways.

The autokinetic effect was a great danger for pilots at night. In early aviation history, pilots would keep in formation in squadrons by staring at the wing light of another plane. Fixating vision at night could lead a pilot to experience the autokinetic effect. He would see a wing light make rapid moves that seemed to show a large change in flight path. The pilot would make quick moves to follow this false path and risked the chance of collisions and spins from which he could crash.

Planes now use bright flashing signal lights, and pilots are trained to keep their eyes moving and not stare while night flying in order to reduce the hazards of the autokinetic effect.

—UNBENDING A CIRCULAR PATH—

A spot of light you know to be moving around the rim of a wheel appears to be moving up and down a hill.

To create this illusion, you'll need luminous tape, the kind that glows in the dark. You can buy it where photography supplies are sold. Pho-

tographers use it to mark light switches and the like in the darkroom. You'll also need some kind of wheel. You can use a bicycle wheel or the wheel on a toy. It's important that this experiment be done in absolute blackness. Put a small square of luminous tape near the rim of the wheel. In a perfectly dark room, roll the wheel across the floor. Watch the luminous tape. In spite of the fact that the tape is traveling around in a circle, its path will make it look as if it's going up and down hill.

If you want to get rid of the illusion, simply put another square of tape at the center of the wheel. When your eyes are looking at two reference points, rather than one, the outside light appears to be traveling around a wheel.

————————ORBITING CIRCLES————————

You can see a drawing of one circle move around another circle that it overlaps. Cut out a five-inch disk from the center of a ten-inch paper plate. Draw two overlapping circles, each one inch in diameter, with black ink as shown. Place the disk on a turntable and stare at one of the circles as it rotates at 33 rpm. The other circle will appear to be moving.

You will not get this effect if you use squares

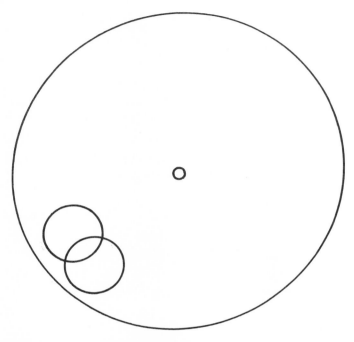

instead of circles. This illusion is partly due to the fact that a circle has no direction. (Squares have corners.) As a result, there are no clues to its rotation. When you stare at one circle, it seems fixed in place. The other circle appears to be gliding around it instead of really changing position.

————THE PHI PHENOMENON————

In this situation *nothing* moves, yet the ap-

pearance of motion is unmistakable. One good
example is a sign of lights, usually in the shape
of an arrow, that seems to be moving in the direction observers should go. There is no confusion
on the part of the customers as to where to
"PARK HERE" or find gas. The secret to this
illusion is the timing of flashing lights.

If two light sources are separated by a short
distance, and one light is flashed on a fraction
of a second after the other flashes off, you see
it as a single source of light that has moved.
You don't see two separate sources of light flashing on and off. This is called the "phi phenomenon," and the appearance of movement depends
on the length of time between stimuli. If the
time between flashing lights is too long, you see
them as separate. Movement is perceived, across
the empty space, when the interval is shortened.
If it is too short, both lights appear to be flashing
simultaneously.

Other senses are also susceptible to the phi
phenomenon. If a light touch is applied to two
nearby points on your skin in rapid sequence,
you will feel as if something moved from one
place to the other. If there is a very short time
interval (a fraction of a second) between a click
heard by one ear and a click heard by the other,
you will sense that the sound has moved through
your head literally in one ear and out the other.

Flip the corners of the pages of this book and see still pictures move. This illusion of motion is based on timing. You must see the sequence very rapidly in order to experience motion.

The image of each drawing is like a flash of light. Psychologists have studied the phenomenon underlying motion pictures and animation by finding out just how fast lights must flash on and off before fusing into a steady beam. The number of flashes per second needed to see flashes as a steady light is called the "critical fusion frequency." The critical fusion frequency varies depending on a number of factors including the brightness of the light and the amount of light versus dark. When the amount of light and dark are equal, dim lights fuse at about 15 flashes per second while bright lights fuse at 60 flashes per second. Fluorescent lights seem like steady light to our eyes, although they are blinking on and off at 60 times per second. If a bright light flashes too slowly, you see flickering.

Motion pictures flash 24 pictures or frames per second. We don't see flickering because there is very little dark between frames. That is, there is a much longer light period compared to dark. If the dark between frames on the film were the same size as a frame, you would see flicker-

ing. And, if the light is too bright or the film is moving too slowly, the movie will flicker.

Films can be used to show other kinds of motion illusions depending on the speeds of the camera and the projector. Slow motion is produced by taking pictures very rapidly and projecting them more slowly than normal. Time-lapse photography speeds up slow events such as the opening of a flower by taking photos over a long period of time, then projecting the frames rapidly.

Animation works on the same principle as motion pictures except that a series of drawings replace frames or photographs. Flip books that work by flipping pages are a simple animation device. An early but more sophisticated animator was a zoetrope. It is a cylinder with slits in it at even intervals. There is a slightly different picture under each slit. When the zoetrope spins, you look through the slits which are traveling past your eyes fast enough to give you a view of images in a series of rapid flashes. Thus the figure moves.

STROBOSCOPIC VISION

Motion enables you to see through something that you can't see through when motionless. You can "see through" the blades of a fan when they are moving, and the slats of a picket fence if you are traveling past them. This "stroboscopic effect," where an interrupted image is fused, is similar to the critical fusion frequency discussed in the last experiment.

An old parlor trick is based on this phenomenon. Draw a grid on a piece of tracing paper as follows. First draw a series of parallel lines that are about ⅛ inch apart with a black pen or pencil. Then draw a second series of parallel lines at right angles to the first. Next draw a series of diagonal lines over the other sets. Finally, draw a fourth set of diagonal lines in the opposite direction.

Place the tracing paper grid over a book and try to read through it. Not a chance! Now give the paper rapid jerks back and forth. Suddenly the words appear and you can read with no trouble.

Stroboscopes are explained and explored in the next experiment.

STOP ACTION

You can make the blades of a fan seem to stop, and you can see a fluorescent light flicker on and off, if you look at them the right way. The way to look at them is with a stroboscope.

Here's how to make one.

Cut out a five-inch disk from the center of a paper plate. Locate the center by folding a similar disk in quarters. Lay the folded disk along the flat one so that the arcs match. Mark the center with a pencil. Trace a faint pencil line from the center to the edge to mark one radius. Cut a slit ⅛ inch wide and one inch long along the radius about ½ inch from the edge.

Use a circular piece of tape (sticky side out) to attach the center of the disk to the end of an electric mixer beater. Observe a fluorescent light or a spinning fan through the slit as you slowly increase the speed of the mixer. (If the mixer doesn't change speeds gradually, begin observing at its fastest speed.) With the proper timing, the bulb will appear to flicker on and off.

You can also see stroboscopic patterns on a television screen. The picture is created by a beam of light that scans the screen in a horizontal direction flashing a series of dark and light spots at extremely high speed. If viewed through a strobe, you can see horizontal bars appear on the screen that appear to move up or down.

Rotating spokes of a wheel also create a stroboscopic effect. So do movies. In addition, all wagon-wheel spokes look the same so you can't tell the order in which they are moving. The combination of these factors produces the unusual effect in movies of making wagon-wheel spokes turn backward while the wagon moves forward.

—BE YOUR OWN STROBOSCOPE—

The illusion we are reporting here we could not experience. It was reported in two scientific journals, however, so there must be something to it. Perhaps you will have better luck than we did. It's so outlandish it's worth a try.

You can make horizontal bars seem to appear on a television screen or make a rotating black and white disk on a turntable seem to stop spinning by humming. The note to hum is around a bass A flat. Apparently this humming makes your retinas vibrate so that the effect is similar to that of a stroboscope, only the illusion is created by your own vibrations in your eyes.

The British scientist who reported this effect hummed while watching a black and white sectored disk on a turntable. He could make the sectors of the disk stop, migrate forward and backward by changing the pitch of the note he hummed. The American scientist who hummed while watching his television screen stood far away from his set (about twenty feet). The hori-

zontal bars he saw migrated up and down as he hummed higher and lower.

————A SUM OF THE PARTS————

Here's where you think you are seeing the whole picture, but you're really looking at only a slice.

Cut a slit in a large piece of cardboard 2 inches long and $\frac{1}{16}$ inch wide. Place the slit over any picture in this book. Move the slit rapidly back and forth over the picture. You'll have a sense that you are seeing the whole thing although you are really only seeing a sequence of $\frac{1}{16}$-inch slices.

Psychologists believe this illusion gives insight into the way our brains process information. The image on the retina is only the slice. But our brain puts the pieces together, and we perceive the complete shape.

————THE NO-HOLES BAR————

A wooden matchstick passes through the steel bar of a safety pin before your very eyes. This is an old parlor trick where it seems that wood passes through steel. This takes a little preparation. Cut the head off a wooden match. Insert the point of a large safety pin through the exact center of the matchstick and close the pin. Move the matchstick over to the center of the pin.

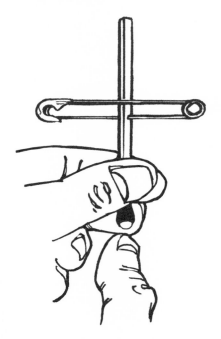

To create the illusion, hold the head of the pin in your left hand (reverse if you're left-handed). Rotate the stick so that the top end is behind the bar of the pin, and the match is turning on the bottom bar of the pin. Strike the bottom end of the match with your right index finger. The top end of the match will appear to

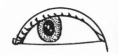

move toward you right through the bar of steel.

Here's what's really happening. By striking downward, you bounce the top end of the matchstick against the upper bar. The lower end moves forward and up. It appears as if the match has moved through the steel bar because the time between the two positions is so rapid that you can't see them separately. Also, your experience with the motion used to strike the match leads you to expect the top part of the stick to move toward you.

FAST MONEY

Rub two coins together and see three! This is not a get-rich-quick scheme. Like most such plans, this too is an illusion.

Get two identical coins. Rub them rapidly up and down against each other with your index fingers as shown in the picture. An image of a third coin drops down between the two real ones.

The phantom coin is caused by a slight afterimage left by the real coins that has not yet had time to fade. The receptors will send messages to your brain after a stimulus is removed for a brief period. By continually moving the coins you keep the afterimage going. Here's a mystery still to be solved: no one knows why the image always appears *below* the real coins, not above.

A wooden pencil suddenly looks like it's made of flexible rubber. The illusion depends on your making the right moves. Here's how. Hold the end of the pencil loosely between your thumb and index finger. Shake your hand rapidly up and down so that the pencil wobbles between your fingers. It will seem to become limp and wavy along its length. You can produce the same effect with a butter knife at the dinner table for after-dinner entertainment.

This is another case where motion produces afterimages on your retinas. The end of the pencil is moving through a wider arc than the middle of the pencil. The combination of afterimages at the end of the pencil and the real image in the center produces the illusion of flexibility.

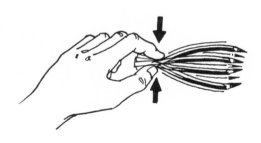

—THE PERVERSE PENDULUM AND—
————FANTASY SPEEDS————

A pendulum you know to be swinging from side to side appears to be moving in an elliptical path. The path has depth because one of your eyes is receiving more light than the other. This effect is known as the Pulfrich phenomenon.

Make a pendulum bob by tying a weight (such as a small saucepan with a hole in the handle) to the end of a three-foot string. Hang the pendulum so that it can swing freely from side to side in front of you. Stand about three feet from the swinging pendulum and cover one eye with the dark lens of a pair of sunglasses. (You can use inexpensive sunglasses that are party favors for little children and cut the glasses in half.) If your right eye is covered, the bob will appear to move toward you as it moves from left to right, and away from you as it moves from right to left. The three-dimensional forward-and-back motion reverses when you observe it with your left eye covered by the dark lens. The entire effect is heightened if you stand on a chair and look down on the bob. The string will appear to grow longer and shorter as the pendulum swings back and forth.

This illusion is apparently due to the difference in reaction between rods and cones. Cones, which are stimulated in bright light, respond more quickly than rods. Your uncovered eye is sending its "message" to your brain sooner than your covered eye. The slight difference in timing is interpreted by your brain the same way as the slight difference in image between left and right eye. Instead of seeing a conflict of two images of the pendulum, one light and one dark, you see depth.

Another illusion demonstrates remarkably how the eyes gauge speed differently when there

is different illumination for each eye. When you are looking out a side window of a moving car, you will appear to be traveling at different speeds depending on which eye is observing the scene through a dark lens. When the leading eye is covered (the one that is in the direction you are moving), you will seem to be traveling much more slowly than when the trailing eye is covered. The illusion of slower speed is accompanied by the illusion of reduced size of familiar objects. Other cars on the road appear smaller than usual. When you have the illusion of increased speed, these same familiar objects appear to be larger than life.

There are individual differences in the perception of this illusion. But it is most intense in dim light, or when you are passing a complicated pattern such as a forest. It is also affected by the speed of the car.

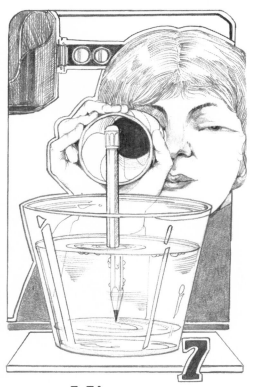

Mirages
and
Other Visual Oddities

We are capable of seeing all kinds of unreal sights. Perhaps the classic example is a mirage— the illusion of water in the distance that lures the thirsty desert traveler to push on and on in

pursuit of a vision that is never reached. Human perception is not completely to blame for such a sight for sore eyes. Mirages are real enough to be photographed. They are caused by the way light is reflected inside rising masses of hot air, producing a shimmering effect easily mistaken for water. Thirst may enhance the illusion, but it is certainly not the principal factor. You can see a mirage when you're not thirsty, too. We'll show you how in this chapter.

There are also visions that are before your eyes all the time that you may not have noticed. These are built into the construction of your eyeball and can be an "insight" to some of the ways your eyes work. Some are sights you can "see" with your eyes closed. Some mean looking deeply into your own eyeballs. We'll show you that, too.

The location of your eyes in the front of your head also gives rise to some peculiar sights. Under the proper conditions you can see holes through solid objects, and you can make two flat pictures combine to form one that has three dimensions.

And, finally, there are the strange effects of "tired" eyes, afterimages of form and color that come from staring at something long enough for your retina to act like film in a camera. When you look elsewhere, the image stays with you for a few minutes before fading.

The eye and nature combine to produce some truly remarkable visual oddities. Be prepared for a sight-seeing tour!

FALSE PONDS

You don't have to be in the Sahara to see a water mirage or false oasis. You can see one on a hot asphalt road on a bright summer day. The best time to look is when you are traveling. Look ahead down the road. When the angle or slope of the road is just right, the roadbed will look wet.

A water mirage, as we mentioned earlier, is caused by the difference between the hot air mass rising over a road and surrounding cooler air. Light traveling through the hot air will be reflected internally in much the same way light is reflected inside a diamond. The internal reflection in a diamond gives the stone its brilliance. Internal reflection in an air mass makes light appear to shimmer. Water in the distance gives a shimmering appearance because of the way light is reflected off its surface, not internally.

Here's another mirage you can look for on a hot summer day. Find a long wall with an even surface. A flat brick wall will do. Put your head against the wall and look down its length. Have

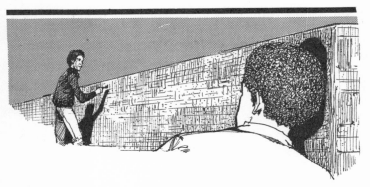

a friend stand next to the wall, about ten yards away, holding a bright shiny object like a key. Watch carefully as your friend brings the key nearer and nearer the wall. The image of the key will appear wavy, and the wall itself will act like a mirror reflecting this wavy image of the key. The air next to the wall is warmer than air further away, thus making the wall act as if it is the shiny wet surface of water, which can produce mirror images.

PRISONER'S CINEMA

Here's how to see the light with your eyes closed. Gently press a closed eyelid with your fingertip. You will see a glowing circle or semi-circle of light directly beneath your finger. Scientists call this sight a *phosphene*, from Greek

— 111 —

words meaning "to show light." If you increase
the pressure of your finger, you'll see more light

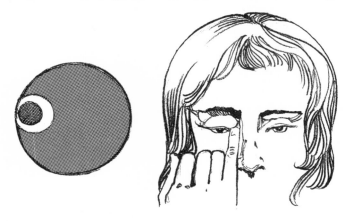

in the form of shimmering geometric patterns.
An especially good way to generate phosphenes
is to close your eyes in the shower, and let water
strike your eyelids.

Pressure is not the only way phosphenes are
produced. In the eighteenth century, people en-
tertained themselves at parties by joining hands,
closing eyes, and receiving a shock from one of
the newly invented electrical generators. Drugs
that produce hallucinations, such as LSD, and
alcohol have been known to cause disturbing
phosphenes in patients recovering from drug de-
pendencies and alcoholism. Stimulation during
brain operations of the vision center of the brain
causes phosphenes. (Very often patients are con-

scious during brain surgery. The brain itself has no pain receptors, so local anesthesia is all that is needed to prevent the sensation of pain in the scalp and skull.) But one of the most interesting cases is the spontaneous occurrence of phosphenes when people have nothing to look at for a period of time. People who lived in dark dungeons reported seeing them—thus giving them the name "prisoner's cinema." Mystics shut off from the world may well be seeing phosphenes when they "see the light" of religious experience. Phosphenes are a hazard to truckers peering into snowstorms for long periods of time. Airplane pilots flying through clouds or at high altitudes during daylight are also susceptible to the annoyance of phosphenes.

Phosphenes are an area of active scientific research. They are caused by the firing of the nerves of vision that usually respond to light stimuli. Their firing when there is no light may be a clue to the orderliness of nerve cells on the retina.

——SPOTS BEFORE YOUR EYES——

Here's a reality you probably overlooked. There are always spots before your eyes. It's just a matter of focusing on them under the right conditions. Make a pinhole in a piece of cardboard. Look through it at a bright source of light. You'll see all kinds of transparent circles floating before your eyes.

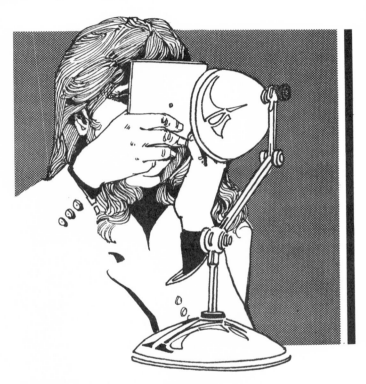

These spots, which are called *floaters*, are actually old blood cells that are floating in the fluid in your eyeballs. They have broken loose from surrounding tissues and swelled into spheres by absorbing some of the fluid within the eye. The

fluid in your eyes is transparent and so are these swollen cells. The pinhole helps you focus on the patterns of light passing through the cell membranes that form the outlines of these floaters.

----------GHOSTLY TREES----------

See a tree on the wall in a dark room. Actually, it's not a tree at all but the shadow of the blood vessels in your eyes. In this experiment you'll look out of the depths of your own eye.

You'll need a flashlight and a dark room. Close one eye and cover it with your hand. Shine the flashlight at the white of the outside of your other eye while you gaze at a blank wall. You might also try blinking the light on and off. After a while, you'll see the image of a leafless "tree" in the dark area of the wall. This tree is an image of the blood vessels on the back of your eye. You can also see them when you first open your eyes in the morning and look at bright sunlight. Before you fully adapt to the bright light, you may catch a glimpse of the shadowy figures of branching blood vessels.

—AN ELEVENTH FINGER AND—
—A ONE-EYED FRIEND—

You can see an eleventh finger, with a fingernail at each end, floating in midair. Put the tips of your index fingers together about a foot away from your eyes. Keep your eyes focused on this spot as you bring your fingers toward your eyes. You'll see a peculiar double-nailed finger appear between the tips of your real fingers just below

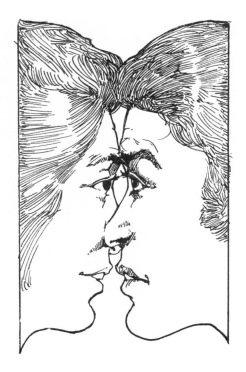

your direct gaze. Draw your fingertips apart, and the eleventh finger will appear to float in midair.

The same kind of look can make a friend appear to have one eye. Look straight ahead and focus on a distant spot while you put your forehead and nose against a friend's. Your friend's eyes will appear to be a single eye in the middle of the forehead.

When you try to look directly at each illusion it disappears. Each eye has a slightly different view of the subject you're looking at. You can see this as double vision by holding up your index finger, pointed at the ceiling about a foot in front of your right eye. If you focus on a spot about three feet away, you'll see a double image of your finger. Most of the time, when you focus on an object, the two images fuse to produce a three-dimensional view. In these examples, by focusing beyond your fingers and your friend's eyes, the images fuse improperly to create these strange sights.

——A HOLE IN YOUR HAND——

See a hole through your hand, a book, a friend's head, or any other solid object. Roll a piece of paper into a tube. Put the tube to one eye and focus both eyes on a distant area at

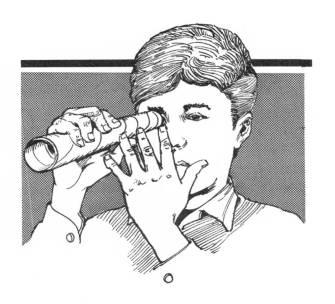

least fifteen feet away. Now bring your hand,
or some other object, up in front of the eye that
is not looking through the tube, still keeping both
eyes on the distant object. Move your hand back
and forth until you find the exact spot where it
appears as if there is a hole in your hand through
which you are looking at the distant object.

This illusion, like the last two, is based on the
fact that your eyes are set apart and see slightly
different images. When your eyes are focused
on a distant object, nearby objects are out of
focus, and the image you see in one eye overlaps
improperly with the image you see in the other.

You can eliminate this illusion of the hole in your hand by focusing both eyes on your hand. Switch back to the distant object, and again you'll have the illusion that your hand contains a bloodless hole.

You can train yourself to ignore the image in one open eye while you concentrate on what you're seeing with the other. Scientists are trained to look through the single ocular of a microscope with both eyes open. Keeping one eye shut when you have to study specimens under the microscope for long periods of time causes eye strain. At first you may be bothered by what you see with the other open eye. But, after a while, you don't even notice those images.

——————HERE'S THE LIMIT——————

These patterns are not identical. One is made up of a single line. The other is made up of two discontinuous sections. Can you tell which is which just by looking at them? We think not. You must trace the pattern carefully to tell which is which.

These figures were designed by two scientists at the Massachusetts Institute of Technology and are named Minsky-Papert figures, after their designers. They show what the limits of pure perception are, because you cannot tell the difference spontaneously but with effort.

The limits of pure perception are of interest to scientists because of what they say about human survival. Scientists think that our inability to perceive certain patterns means that such discriminations were not crucial to the survival of early man.

For example, survival of early man depended on his being able to see a predator against a natural background. If the predator had a natural camouflage that was outside our perceptual limits, we could be in big trouble. It is crucial to see one's enemy! Experiments with patterns like these establish these limits. Then anthropologists, and other scientists, can apply this information. Perhaps if we could not see a particular predator, it was not a threat to us.

Here's how you can put this drawing of a bird in the drawing of the cage. Stare at the bird for thirty seconds in bright light. Then gaze at the cage. An afterimage of a black bird will appear in the cage.

Look at the cover of this book, then at the dot in the green heart surrounded by a yellow border for thirty seconds. Now stare at a white background. An afterimage of a red heart surrounded by a blue border will appear.

In general, afterimages are caused by continued firings of receptor cells in the eye after being stimulated. There are two kinds of afterimages, positive and negative. The examples we've just given are both negative afterimages. They are produced while the eye is adjusting to the stimulus. The color of an afterimage is explained by a theory that the same receptors share red-green stimulation, while different receptors share blue-yellow stimulation. When you are looking at green, the red part of the receptor is shut down. If there is a long exposure to the green stimulus, removing it allows the red afterimage to appear.

A positive afterimage is caused by a brief exposure to a bright light in an eye previously adjusted to less illumination. You have experienced a positive afterimage when you see a flashbulb or gaze briefly into the sun. The positive afterimage quickly changes to a negative one.

—CIRCLES FROM STRAIGHT LINES—

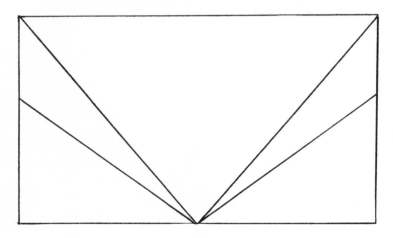

Straight lines become concentric circles when you spin them. Motion plus afterimages produce this illusion.

Copy the four black lines in the diagram onto a 3" x 5" unlined index card. Spin it at its center on a pen or pencil point. The lines become concentric circles spinning about one another.

You get an interesting effect if you spin the disk shown below. Make a photocopy of it and

cut it out, or trace it onto a white disk. Rotate the disk slowly on a turntable. Notice how the lines become blurred in sections. You can also rotate the disk at high speeds on the end of an electric mixer beater. (We attached ours with a sticky circle of tape at the center of the underside of the disk.) At high speeds all the lines become concentric circles. It seems that our eyes tend to focus all the black of the line at some central point. Since each line is a different distance from the center, the concentration of black forms a circular pattern.

─────────PEPPER'S GHOST─────────

The last few illusions in this chapter have nothing to do with the way you perceive things. They are created by the way light interacts with surfaces and transparent substances. Pepper's Ghost is an old stage trick which you can recreate in miniature so that a candle appears to be burning in a glass of water. You will need a flat sheet of glass or Plexiglas (we used the removable cover for a turntable), a glass of water, a candle in a holder, and a barrier made by a stack of books.

This works best in a dimly lit area. Set up

the glass on an angle at one side of the stack of books. Put the glass of water behind it. Now light the candle and place it behind the barrier so that it can't be seen from the front. If you maneuver the candle and glass correctly, the candle will appear to be burning in the glass of water.

Here's what's really happening. The glass is material that does two things. First, it allows light to pass through it so you can see the glass of water behind it. Second, its surface also reflects the image of the candle. This trick was used in the theater. An actor offstage cast a reflection on an invisible glass surface. It appeared that the actor was walking through doors and furniture as if he were a ghost.

DISTORTED IMAGES

See a straight pencil look bent, the image of a coin on the surface of a glass of water, and the shadow of a broken pencil. These illusions are all caused by refraction, or the bending of light as it passes from one transparent substance—water—to another—air.

Here's how to create the illusions. Hold a pencil partially submerged in water. If you look at it from the side, it will appear to be bent where it enters the water. This illusion makes people look as though they have especially short legs

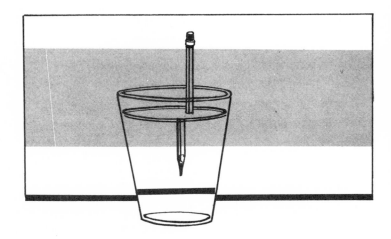

when they are standing in a swimming pool. Light rays are bent as they pass the boundary between water and air toward the surface of the water. As a result, the object they are coming from appears to be higher than it actually is. The bottom surface appears shallower than it really is, people appear foreshortened, and the pencil point appears closer. A coin on the bottom of a glass of water appears to be at the surface because the back surface of the glass acts like a mirror with a reflected image which is refracted.

Hold a pencil in a basin of water so that it is partially submerged. Look at the shadow cast at the bottom. It will be broken into two segments. The reason is that water at the surface clings to the pencil, curving upward. Light that would be a part of the shadow is refracted by this curved surface, so that it is no longer part of the shadow.

————A FLATTENED SUN————

Ever notice how the sun looks slightly oval when it is about to set? No, the sun really isn't flatter. Its image is being bent by our atmosphere in the same way that water bends the image of a stick. The lower the sun on the horizon, the greater the bending of its rays. Light coming from the top of the sun's disk is refracted, so it appears to be higher than it actually is. Your eye assumes it to be where it sees it. A ray coming from the bottom of the sun has to pass through more of the atmosphere because of its lower position, thus it is bent more. So the bottom of the sun is higher than the top, giving the setting sun a flatter shape.

Great Misconceptions

For centuries people believed that their senses gave a true picture of the earth and its place in the universe. This is entirely understandable given the nature of human perception. Then evi-

dence turned up suggesting that some well-accepted notions were incorrect. Arguments arose defending established views. Some challenges took on powerful institutions, such as the Catholic Church, when they stated different opinions. Sometimes there was violence. In 1600, Giordano Bruno, an Italian philosopher, was put to death for unconventional views. Traditional ideas die hard even in the face of overwhelming evidence.

Science gradually destroyed the misconceptions about the earth and the workings of the natural world. Scientists arrive at large, general conclusions out of many specific bits of information. They establish the truth of many facts related to an event or concept. When enough facts have been collected, a general statement is made. In the last three hundred years scientists have amassed reliable information, enabling us to know much truth about nature. Scientific instruments have extended the range and accuracy of our senses. Scientific experiments have lessened the likelihood of judgments based on prejudice or emotions. Science "sees through" the built-in handicaps of our perception. And in the future, as we make use of the scientific procedures to study ourselves, we may learn to understand our perceptions better.

Once we looked at the world differently, and

what we thought we saw turned out to be wrong. This chapter tells the stories of some popular illusions that fooled almost everyone. If you had lived in the past, no doubt you, too, would have been fooled.

THE EARTH IS FLAT

Today everyone knows that the earth is a sphere. Actually, we accept this idea rather blindly; it's hard to imagine that anyone ever thought differently. But five hundred years ago most people thought the earth was flat. Why?

Because it looked flat. Popular opinion was that the earth was shaped like a round pancake. Land

was surrounded by ocean, and a ship would sail off the edge of the earth at the horizon.

Of course, the evidence that the earth was a sphere always existed if anyone cared to look for it. About 500 B.C. a Greek philosopher named Pythagoras and his followers said that the earth was a sphere. They didn't give any proof, but their views were well thought out. They obviously had reason to believe the earth was not flat. Two hundred years later, Aristotle backed up Pythagoras. During an eclipse of the moon, he observed that the shadow of the earth was visible on the surface of the moon. This shadow,

Aristotle noted, was always a perfect curve. If the earth was any shape other than a sphere, he concluded, the shadow would not always be such a perfect curve.

There is other evidence in the heavens for careful observers. When a person travels south toward the equator, the north star (among others) appears to move lower in the sky. At the equator, the north star is on the horizon, and south of the equator you can't see it at all. If the earth were flat, the north star would always be the same height above the horizon no matter how far south you traveled.

Finally, there is the truth of what really happens to ships when they reach the horizon. You can see for yourself, if you are near the sea. Ships seem to disappear, as if they have dropped off the edge of the earth. First, the hull disappears, then the superstructure, finally the masts.

But if you take the trouble to watch for ships on the horizon, you will find that they appear from top to bottom in the reverse order. First you'd see the top of the masts, then the structures on deck, and finally the hull.

All of these observations are indirect evidence for the earth having a curved surface, its curve so large that it appeared flat to human eyes. True proof only came when people sailed around the world. Columbus set off in 1492 to do this. He believed he could find a new route to India by sailing west. His attempt was halted with the discovery of the Americas. About thirty years later, the task was accomplished. One of the ships in Magellan's fleet returned to Spain after a three-year voyage.

Photographs of the earth from space leave no doubt that the earth is a sphere, if anyone is still around to challenge the idea. A person who today insists on believing his or her personal perceptions and refuses to acknowledge the earth is round may well be considered crazy. Five hundred years ago believers in a round earth were in the small minority. They were considered the lunatics.

THE EARTH IS THE CENTER OF THE UNIVERSE

If you spend some time watching the sky, you will observe that there is motion in the heavens. Every day, the sun rises in the east, moves across the sky, and sets in the west. The moon also rises and sets, as do the stars. The position of the star pattern in the dome of the night sky changes over the year. But when the year is up, the stars are back in the same place they were the year before. The paths of bright bodies called planets also wander across the sky. Their route is not quite as regular as the sun, moon, and stars. Occasionally they appear to move backward before moving forward again. But if you spend a long enough time studying the motion of the planets, sooner or later they will return to the spot where you first noticed them. For certain planets, the return to their starting point takes years.

The first person to study the motions of heavenly bodies systematically was a Greek astronomer named Ptolemy, who was born about seventy-five years after Christ. He devised a system of the heavens as he saw it. The earth was motionless, and sun, moon, planets, and stars revolved around it. His system was good enough

to predict future positions of the heavenly bodies with as much accuracy as could be viewed with the naked eye, for there were no telescopes. Ptolemy's system was so successful it became the official position of the most powerful political and spiritual organization in Europe at that time, the Catholic Church.

The earth-centered concept of the universe was the accepted view for well over one thousand years. But even during this time, small inconsistencies not predicted by Ptolemy kept cropping up. Adjustments were made in the system by adding more circles to the paths of the planets, and the Ptolemaic view became more and more complicated. In the sixteenth century a new concept of the universe was proposed by Nicolaus Copernicus, a Polish churchman. He had spent over thirty years observing and measuring the motions of the planets and stars. His observations were extremely accurate, even without a telescope. Copernicus proposed a system with the sun at the center and the earth simply another planet that moved around it. He proposed that the earth had two kinds of motion. It moved around the sun and it also rotated on its axis like a top. In the Copernican system the inconsistencies in the Ptolemaic theory were cleared up. The plan was beautifully simple. But by believing that it was the earth that moved Copernicus challenged common sense, and, more dangerous, the official position of the church. He had no direct evidence that the earth was, in fact, moving.

Copernicus knew his idea would cause trouble. He anticipated some of the objections that would be raised. There was an argument that a moving earth would leave behind birds in flight. Copernicus answered that birds and the atmosphere moved along with the earth. There was an argument that the positions of the stars would change against a pattern of background stars if the earth was changing its position. This is the idea of parallax you saw for yourself when you looked at an object with each eye. The position of a nearby object changes in relation to the background because each eye sees it from a slightly different position. Star patterns of closer stars should change, relative to background stars, when seen from different positions of the earth in its orbit around the sun at different times of the year. Copernicus's answer was that the distances between the earth and the stars were so great that there was no noticeable change in star patterns. Years after Copernicus's death, measurements through the telescope revealed the expected parallax.

Copernicus feared the all-powerful church would reject his ideas, so he dedicated his great book, *On the Revolutions of the Spheres*, to the

Pope. It was a political move. He had even hesitated to have his book published at all, saying, "I feared I would be laughed off the stage." He did not see a printed and bound copy of his book until he was on his deathbed. As Copernicus expected, the church did reject his system, and his book was put on the list of books that people were forbidden to read. The few people who believed in his system put their careers on the line, even their lives. Giordano Bruno, the Italian philosopher mentioned earlier, in 1600 was burned at the stake for supporting the Copernican view of the solar system.

The support that directly led to the acceptance of the Copernican system came almost one hundred years later. Galileo Galilei (1564–1642), an Italian mathematician and astronomer, refined the telescope and made some amazing discoveries. Among them was the observation of the moons of Jupiter revolving around that planet. This was obvious proof that not everything revolved (according to the church), around the earth. Galileo presented his arguments for the Copernican system in a popular and witty book. His arguments were so convincing that the church called him a heretic and put his book on its forbidden list. Galileo was brought to trial, publicly condemned, forced to recant his opinion, and sentenced to life imprisonment. But the word was out. And it has stood the tests of time and all additional information about the universe.

-OBJECTS COME TO REST IN THEIR-
————NATURAL PLACE————

Up until the fifteenth century, Aristotle's view of the natural world was the one accepted by educated people. Aristotle based his opinions on his observations, which were subject to error as he was only human. His concept of motion may well have been his greatest misconception. According to Aristotle, all matter was made up of four elements: earth, air, fire, and water. All matter possessed one or more of these elements and each element had its natural place. Fire was highest, air was under fire, water was under air, and earth was at the bottom. All objects would move to their "natural" place depending on the elements they possessed. Thus, fire rises through air, air rises through water, and earth falls through all three.

There was a lot of common sense to support Aristotle. Water bubbles up through earth. If you add fire to water, steam forms which rises through air. When steam loses some of its fire, it falls back on to the earth as water. In addition to their "natural" motion of moving to their place

of rest, objects could also have violent motion as a result of some event. Throwing a stone gives the stone violent motion for a while. When the stone loses its violent motion, natural motion takes over until it returns to its natural place. Nice theory, if you don't look too closely.

In the sixteenth century Aristotle's views on motion were questioned. In the seventeenth century, they were put to rest by Galileo, whose examination of motion made him "the father of modern physics." Galileo not only challenged the idea that all objects move to their "natural" place of rest, but that rest itself is a natural state. He claimed that an object in motion should remain in motion forever under ideal circumstances. Such an idea of continuing motion on earth is hard to imagine, even today. Moving objects on earth, if left alone, eventually do come to rest.

To back up his idea, Galileo presented a "thought experiment" which is an example of logic at its best. Here is his basic argument.

1. When a ball rolls down a hill, it rolls faster and faster.

2. If you give a ball a shove so that it rolls up a hill, it rolls more and more slowly, until it comes to a brief stop before rolling back down a hill.

Conclusion: A ball rolling on level ground

should not pick up speed or lose speed. It should keep rolling at the same speed forever. That it does *not* keep rolling is due to an additional factor.

Galileo correctly figured that friction in the real world prevented balls from rolling forever. He put us on the road to a true understanding of motion which now states some external force is the cause of a *change* in either a state of motion or a state of rest. He removed forever the idea that inanimate objects had a "desire" to return to their natural place.

—HEAVY OBJECTS FALL FASTER—

Aristotle really went out on a limb when he said, ". . . [if] one weight is twice as heavy as another, it will take half as long to fall. . . ." Obviously trusting his senses, there is no evidence that Aristotle ever tested this idea. Galileo did and proved, contrary to what you might think, that regardless of weight all bodies fall at the same speed.

There is a legend that Galileo checked this out in a public demonstration, dropping unequal weights off the leaning tower of Pisa. There is no evidence that he actually performed this test, although he wrote of such an experiment. He pointed out that the two objects would arrive at the ground at almost the same time. If there were a small difference in impact, it was not as important as the closeness of arrival time.

Galileo had problems in studying falling bodies because there were no accurate timing devices.

He ingeniously got around this problem by creating a kind of slow-motion device for falling objects. He rolled balls down slanted boards. He reasoned that the change in speed of a rolling ball was similar to its change in speed when falling freely. Thus Galileo was able to measure distance and time, two quantities of speed, and give conclusive evidence that all objects fall at the same rate (if there is no resistance from the air) regardless of their weight.

The experiment was repeated on the moon,

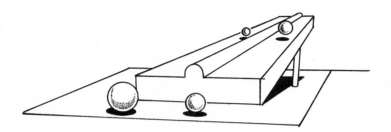

where there is no atmosphere to interfere. Sure enough, a feather and a golf ball reached the ground at the same time.

About the Author

VICKI COBB attended the University of Wisconsin on a Ford Foundation Early Admissions Scholarship, then continued her education at Barnard College, where she received her B.A. degree, and at Columbia University Teachers College, where she was awarded an M.A. degree.

After an early career as a science teacher, Ms. Cobb turned to writing. In addition to film strips and other educational aids, she has written scripts for network television, and was the creator and principal personality of "The Science Game," an educational television series. Ms. Cobb is the author of a number of books for young people, most of which are on scientific subjects.